SACRAMENTO PUBLIC LIBRARY

D0767877

WITHDRAWN FROM
CIRCULATION

POWERPOINT®
PRESENTATIONS
THAT SELL

POWERPOINT®
PRESENTATIONS
THAT SELL

ADAM B. COOPER

McGraw-Hill

New York   Chicago   San Francisco   Lisbon   London   Madrid   Mexico City
Milan   New Delhi   San Juan   Seoul   Singapore   Sydney   Toronto

The *McGraw·Hill* Companies

Copyright © 2009 by Adam Cooper. All rights reserved. Printed in the United States of America. Except as permitted under the United States Copyright Act of 1976, no part of this publication may be reproduced or distributed in any form or by any means, or stored in a data base or retrieval system, without the prior written permission of the publisher.

1 2 3 4 5 6 7 8 9 0   FGR/FGR   0 1 0 9

ISBN: 978-0-07-162680-4
MHID: 0-07-162680-8

This publication is designed to provide accurate and authoritative information in regard to the subject matter covered. It is sold with the understanding that the publisher is not engaged in rendering legal, accounting, or other professional service. If legal advice or other expert assistance is required, the services of a competent professional person should be sought.

> —*From a declaration of principles jointly adopted by a committee of the American Bar Association and a committee of publishers.*

McGraw-Hill books are available at special quantity discounts to use as premiums and sales promotions, or for use in corporate training programs. To contact a representative please e-mail us at bulksales@mcgraw-hill.com.

To Mom, Dad, and my Anna

Outline of book's modules and chapters

Simple techniques to plan, design, and deliver presentations that get results

Acknowledgments

I never thought this project, which started out as a few notes jotted down during a flight to Guatemala, would result in a published book. Had it not been for the support and encouragement of colleagues, friends, and family, it would not have happened.

I would first like to thank the team at McGraw-Hill for keeping an open mind about writing an entire book as an actual PowerPoint presentation (I think it's a first!). In particular, a great thanks to my editing team of Donya Dickerson and Pattie Amoroso for guiding me through the entire editing process and always being open and honest with me.

I'm extremely grateful to my colleague Gene Zelazny. This book would not exist without his encouragement. A great thanks for providing guidance on numerous rounds of my manuscript. I would not have made it through this process without his mentorship.

A very special thanks to my friends Serge Grossman for reviewing my manuscript on multiple occasions, and to Mike Ehrenberg for offering his opinions and ideas on the book's content and for navigating the publishing process. Many thanks also to Lindsey Engel, Kim Myers, and Scott Schuman for providing their ideas.

I owe thanks most of all to my parents, Bob and Eileen, and my love, Anna. Mom, Dad, thank you so much for being there for me at all hours, supporting everything I do without hesitation, and offering the simplest of encouragement: "just do your best." Anna, thank you for putting up with me getting up at odd hours when inspiration hit and for just being great—love you always.

Chapter 1 Introduction: Creating Presentations That Sell

Experience can be a double-edged sword. In the workplace, it is often what you need to gain confidence in using a specific tool such as a business system or more traditional software such as Microsoft PowerPoint. However, gaining experience takes time, and time is at a premium in today's workplace, where things are expected to be delivered faster with a leaner staff and fewer training resources available to employees.

This book seeks to close the experience gap and bring you up to speed on the fundamentals of using PowerPoint and other similar presentation products to sell your ideas more effectively. This book will give you a set of simple techniques to plan, design, and deliver presentations that get results and get you noticed among your peers and managers. You do not need to have experience with PowerPoint to pick up this book and immediately put its lessons to use.

This book is written from the perspective of someone giving advice over your shoulder to serve as a guiding hand as you begin to organize your project's activities and then ultimately create a PowerPoint presentation. Regardless of what part of an organization you belong to or are considering joining, you can use this book at any stage of a project and learn slide structuring techniques and speed shortcut tips that are instantly applicable. The book offers both conceptual and tactical approaches to plan, design, and deliver presentations that get results (see Figure 1–1).

As you can see in Figure 1–1, the pages in the rest of the book after this introduction are written as an actual PowerPoint presentation. This reinforces the book's recommendations on every single page (the book practices what it preaches). I believe it is easier to learn new ideas when they are in the form of the desired end product. Thus, it is easier to learn about creating better presentations by using a book written as a presentation. Whether

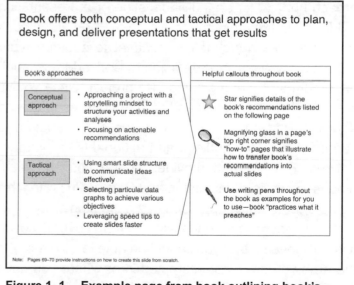

Book offers both conceptual and tactical approaches to plan, design, and deliver presentations that get results

Book's approaches	Helpful callouts throughout book
Conceptual approach — • Approaching a project with a storytelling mindset to structure your activities and analyses • Focusing on actionable recommendations	⭐ Star signifies details of the book's recommendations listed on the following page
	🔍 Magnifying glass in a page's top right corner signifies "how-to" pages that illustrate how to transfer book's recommendations into actual slides
Tactical approach — • Using smart slide structure to communicate ideas effectively • Selecting particular data graphs to achieve various objectives • Leveraging speed tips to create slides faster	✒ Use writing pens throughout the book as examples for you to use—book "practices what it preaches"

Note: Pages 69–70 provide instructions on how to create this slide from scratch.

Figure 1–1. Example page from book outlining book's approaches and helpful callouts

you're just starting a new job, working on a new project, or have a meeting at the end of the week, this book will help you create presentations with confidence.

This book also is intended to serve as a combined PowerPoint tutorial and business communications resource. Similar to a basic how-to book, it will offer tips and tricks on how to format slides, create objects (e.g., shapes, text boxes, and data graphs), and use helpful shortcut keys. It then goes a step further and provides recommendations on how these slides and objects can be organized to emphasize your story within a slide and across a presentation.

This book is structured to give you a start-to-finish approach not just for an individual slide or a presentation but for an entire project. For example, Part I of the book helps you use a storytelling mindset to structure your project's activities more efficiently and address audience needs at the beginning of a project. Once you've structured your activities and started your research and analysis, Part II helps you use smart slide structure to communicate your findings and actionable recommendations. Part III then provides speed tips and techniques to create slides faster, and Part IV illustrates this entire start-to-finish approach in a case study.

You do not have to read this book from cover to cover. It is designed so that you should be able to go directly to the area you are most interested in or where you have the most immediate need and instantly apply what you

have learned. For example, if you want to understand how to

- **Improve presentation of data,** refer to Chapters 6 through 8, which help you decide which graph type to use, create graphs from scratch, and improve the formatting of the way the data is presented.
- **Learn speed techniques,** refer to Chapter 9, which details instructions on finding and using speed toolbars.
- **Create and/or edit shapes and text boxes,** refer to Chapter 10, which provides step-by-step instructions.
- **Improve slide structure,** refer to Chapter 5, which outlines how to structure a slide's content.
- **Save time during the project,** refer to Chapters 3 and 4 to learn how to use a storytelling mindset and storyboarding to structure your project's activities more efficiently.

As you can see, you can pick up this book at the beginning of a project to help structure your activities, again when you're trying to decide how your project's findings link together as a single coherent story, and then when you're working on the final slides.

This book will bring any PowerPoint user up to speed, allowing you to take full advantage of what PowerPoint has to offer. Pick up the book at different stages of your presentation preparation and practice its recommendations to become more proficient at creating presentations to sell your ideas more effectively.

Chapter 2 How to Use This Book to Get Results

Simple techniques to plan, design, and deliver presentations that get results

Book offers both conceptual and tactical approaches to plan, design, and deliver presentations that get results

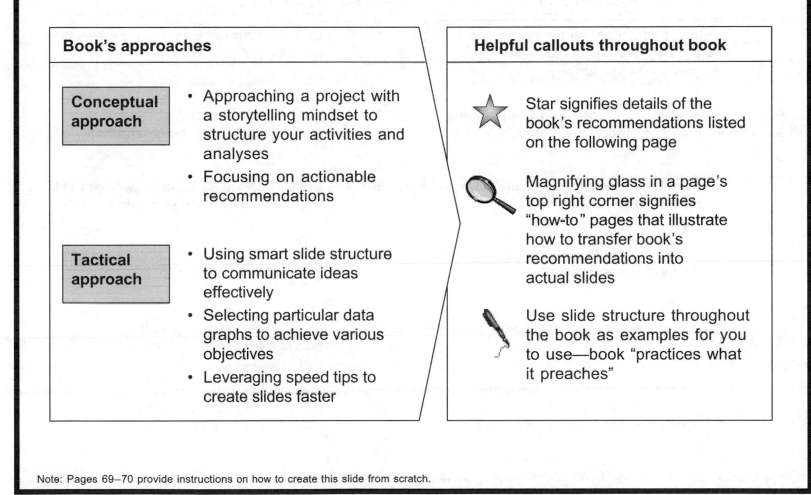

Book's approaches

Conceptual approach	• Approaching a project with a storytelling mindset to structure your activities and analyses • Focusing on actionable recommendations
Tactical approach	• Using smart slide structure to communicate ideas effectively • Selecting particular data graphs to achieve various objectives • Leveraging speed tips to create slides faster

Helpful callouts throughout book

Star signifies details of the book's recommendations listed on the following page

Magnifying glass in a page's top right corner signifies "how-to" pages that illustrate how to transfer book's recommendations into actual slides

Use slide structure throughout the book as examples for you to use—book "practices what it preaches"

Note: Pages 69–70 provide instructions on how to create this slide from scratch.

Book's conceptual and tactical recommendations

	High-level recommendation	Page with details	Try to avoid . . .
Conceptual	⭐1 **Think of your final slide presentation as the communication of your project's end product**	p. 19	Do NOT start thinking about presentation a week before your meeting
	⭐2 **Outline areas of research at beginning of project to focus your analyses**	p. 30	Do NOT start the project by analyzing every piece of information you have
	⭐3 **Handwrite slide drafts on paper before approaching the computer**	p. 39	Do NOT create slides in PowerPoint until you think about slide structure on paper
Tactical	⭐4 **Structure the content on a slide from left to right (when possible)**	p. 54	Do NOT use only bullets and dashes in a top-to-bottom structure
	⭐5 **Write your key learnings directly on the slide**	p. 80	Do NOT just refer to your learnings as talking points
	⭐6 **Reuse slides you previously created for new presentations to save time**	p. 136	Do NOT start from scratch when beginning a new presentation

PowerPoint Presentations That Sell

Book addresses criticisms of how PowerPoint is used

Primary criticisms of how PowerPoint is used

- Slide presentations *do not focus enough on recommended actions* (and focus too much on a collection of analyses or generic thoughts)

Need to focus on *ACTION* throughout

Use the book's strategies to overcome these issues through actionable storytelling to maximize the effectiveness of your slides

- Information and data are often presented in silos with no clear connection, creating a *difficult environment in which to follow the key messages*

Need to use a *STORYTELLING* mindset

Start by embracing the two presentation truths on the following pages

Embrace Presentation Truth 1:
An idea presented on a slide can be more influential than verbal or e-mail communication*

1. What you can do about it

A short set of slides or even a one-slide presentation can go a long way:

- Rather than sending your manager or team an idea by e-mail, write a one-page PowerPoint slide that illustrates why your idea is a good one with supporting rationale

- Print out the slide and walk your manager through the logic in person

Presentation Truth

Since a presentation is one of the final documents used before proceeding with execution, it is easier to convince decision makers to proceed with your idea if it is drafted in PowerPoint rather than in an e-mail or verbal communication

2. Why this is more efficient

- A short set of slides or a one-slide presentation has more sticking power than an e-mail or a one-off discussion

- The slide allows your manager to visualize how the idea can be communicated to the next level up—and gives him or her the means to do so

- Also, this allows for easier "idea iteration"—as the idea evolves over time, you can build a stronger story around the existing slide while saving time

* This is a generalization and is not necessarily relevant for every situation.

Embrace Presentation Truth 2:
Your presentation will be viewed after you initially present it

1. What you can do about it

Create your presentation so that it can live on its own (i.e., without you orally presenting it)

- Make sure all your key messages or "learnings" are written on each slide and not just in your speaking notes

- Learnings should focus on action items resulting from presented material (more details about presenting your learnings appear in Part II)

Presentation Truth

Even after the initial presentation, your PowerPoint slides often will be e-mailed or shown to others in (or outside) the organization, who are probably less familiar with the topic

2. Why this is more efficient

- For your initial audience, it is always helpful to be explicit about the recommended actions and interesting points on each slide so that the audience can both hear and read what matters to your story

- For future readers, it reduces the number of questions you may get as well as providing more value to their work because they can comprehend your story more quickly

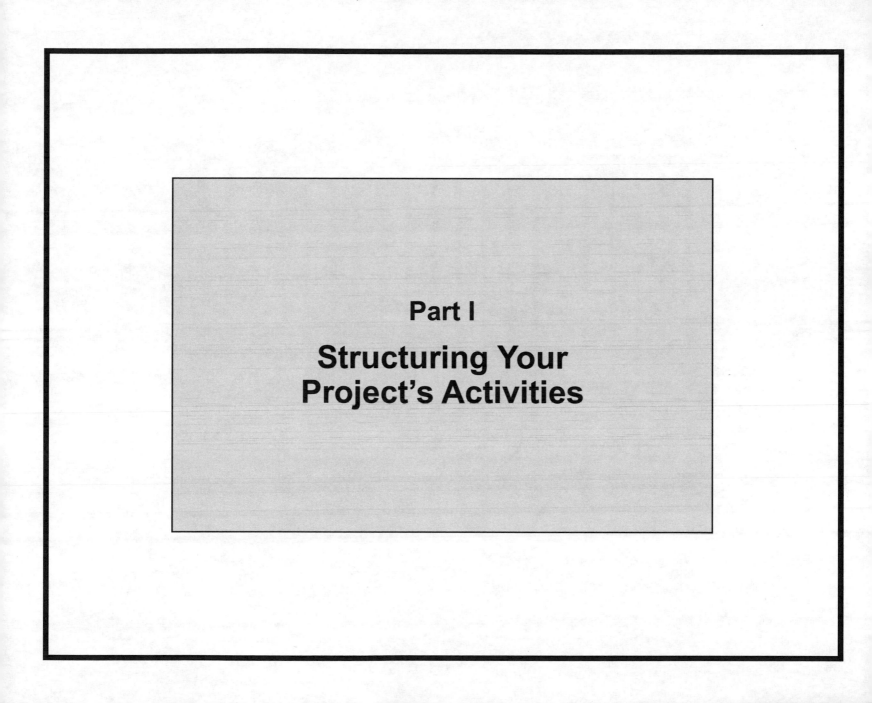

Part I

Structuring Your Project's Activities

Chapter 3 Save Time by Using a Storytelling Mindset

As discussed in the Chapter 1 introduction, the book is structured in three parts, followed by a case study so that you can test and apply what you have learned in your own project setting. Part I focuses on structuring your project's activities and presentation more effectively. Often the most challenging part of a project is knowing where to start! Chapter 3 shows how to use a storytelling mindset to structure a project's activities and analyses from Day 1, before you even turn on the computer. This is extremely valuable because it forces you to think through what the decision makers in the presentation meeting will need to be convinced of and guide your thinking toward this end at the very onset of a project. In other words, what is "mission-critical" to this project? What information will you have to gather and then present to meet expectations? The storytelling approach helps you map this out from the beginning of a project so that you are working efficiently and are focused from the onset on the major deliverables.

Several techniques are introduced to help you use a storytelling mindset in the following chapter. One way to do this is to *agendicize* your project's story. To agendicize means to write out a list of research areas you want to investigate during a project. Creating this list helps structure your thoughts at the onset of a project and keeps you focused on which items are critical throughout the project. It also helps you work efficiently, as it can prevent you from investing large amounts of time in collecting data that is not relevant or of primary importance to the project.

Using a storytelling mindset helps you focus on action . . .

"The power of storytelling is also central to my work as a business executive. . . . I've learned that the **ability to articulate your story is crucial** in almost every phase of enterprise management."

"For the leader, **storytelling is action oriented**—a force for turning dreams into goals and then into results."

"Storytelling can be used to **get people's help carrying out your goals** and ultimately to inspire business success."

Peter Gruber, Entertainment industry executive
HBR, December 2007

"If you're dealing with a **storytelling medium, which is a mechanized means of producing and presenting a dream** that you're inviting people to share, you'd better believe your dream or else it's going to come off as patronizing."

Brad Bird, Oscar-winning director
McKinsey Quarterly, April 2008

Source: Peter Gruber, "The Four Truths of the Storyteller," *Harvard Business Review,* December 2007; Hayagreeva Rao, Robert Sutton, and Allen P. Webb, "Innovation Lessons from Pixar: An Interview with Oscar-Winning Director Brad Bird," *McKinsey Quarterly,* April 2008.

. . . and helps influence others by engaging emotions, making it an effective selling tool

"A good story helps you **influence the interpretation people give to facts**."

"Difference between giving an example and storytelling is **addition of emotional content**."

Annette Simmons
The Story Factor

"**Analysis might excite the mind but it hardly offers a route to the heart**. And that is where leaders have to go to motivate people to spark rapid action with energy and enthusiasm.

"Great leaders have instinctively known [that] **stories inspire and persuade**. The choice for managers is whether to use storytelling (a) unwittingly and clumsily or (b) intelligently and skillfully.

"**Storytelling is a phenomenon that is fundamental to all nations, societies and cultures**, and has been so since time immemorial."

Stephen Denning, business narrative expert
Financial Times, May 2004

"**Storytelling can be an effective business tool**. 'People just don't simply hear stories,' said Joseph L. Badaracco Jr., a business ethics professor at Harvard Business School. 'It triggers things—pictures, thoughts and associations—in their minds. **That makes the stories more powerful and engaging**.'"

Harvard Business School professor
New York Times, November 2000

Source: Annette Simmons, *The Story Factor,* 2nd ed. New York: Basic Books, 2006; Jeffrey L. Seglin, "Storytelling Only Works If Tales Are True," *New York Times,* November 19, 2000; Stephen Denning, "Storytelling Is a Fundamental Skill for Management," *Financial Times.* May 24, 2004.

But people spend most of their time collecting information rather than crafting a story

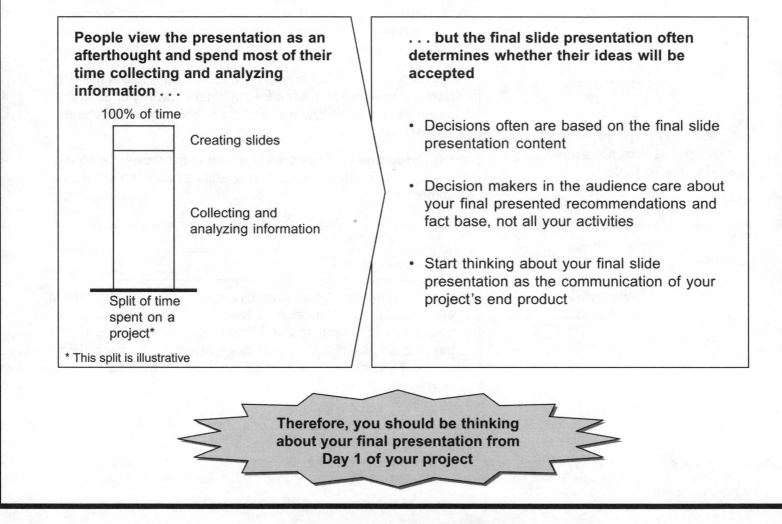

People view the presentation as an afterthought and spend most of their time collecting and analyzing information . . .

100% of time

Creating slides

Collecting and analyzing information

Split of time spent on a project*

* This split is illustrative

. . . but the final slide presentation often determines whether their ideas will be accepted

- Decisions often are based on the final slide presentation content

- Decision makers in the audience care about your final presented recommendations and fact base, not all your activities

- Start thinking about your final slide presentation as the communication of your project's end product

Therefore, you should be thinking about your final presentation from Day 1 of your project

Start thinking about your final slide presentation as the communication of your project's end product

Stop diving right into the information/data collection and analyses before thinking about the slide presentation

Stop waiting to think about your slide presentation until just a few days before the meeting

Use the storytelling mindset described in the next pages to help organize your project activities around your final presentation to become more effective at selling your ideas

The storytelling mindset helps you think through four key story elements

1. Setting the context

Defines the situation that has led you to take on a project and outlines the project's objective

4. Delivering your opinion

Provides the viewpoint you're trying to sell as the outcome of the project

Four key elements of storytelling mindset

2. Connecting emotions

Introduces the needs and opinions of your project's audience (i.e., anyone affected by the outcome of the project) into your activities

3. Providing the facts

Details the information you collect and analyses that support your opinion

These elements benefit the way you manage the overall project . . .

Benefits for managing *overall project*

Setting the context	• Ensures that you identify a clear objective for the project and establish a set of key questions to answer
Connecting emotions	• Forces you to think through the needs of the project's end audience before deciding which activities to pursue
Providing the facts	• Helps you think about which pieces of information will answer the key questions outlined in the context
Delivering your opinion	• Draws out insights from facts that answer the project's key questions

. . . and the way you manage the final slide presentation

Benefits for managing *final slide presentation*

Setting the context	• Explains to the audience how project fits within the group's goals and/or activities (new information/trends that suggest the need to pursue this project)
Connecting emotions	• Influences which information and insights you present on the slides and in speaker notes (level of detail to include)
Providing the facts	• Creates the rationale for your opinion and final recommendations
Delivering your opinion	• Provides the audience with your viewpoint, based on insights from the facts

PowerPoint Presentations That Sell

Now you can use your story to structure your project's activities

2. "Agendicize" your project (detailed later in this chapter)
Create areas of research to focus your efforts on the most important aspects of the project that will encourage decision makers to proceed with your ideas

1. Storytelling mindset
Think through the project's overall objective, key questions, and potential answers (i.e., "your story") *at the very beginning of the project* to guide the way you construct your activities, analyses, and eventual presentation

3. Collect information and analyze
Use agendicized research areas to guide which information to collect and which data to analyze (more efficient than unfocused analysis) and then identify actionable insights

4. Revisit assumptions and update
Continually challenge your assumptions by using data analyses and update your story and activities, as necessary, to create actionable recommendations from the collection of insights

Begin by identifying the project's objective, based on the type of presentation you'll be giving

Type of presentation	Description	Example objectives for presentation
SELLING information	• A "selling" presentation is meant to persuade the audience to adopt a particular point of view • Your position often is supported with options to inform your audience of pros and cons and a rationale for why it should proceed with your ideas	• Create a business plan for a new product or service launch and get sign-off from management • Identify and prioritize new opportunities • Request funding for the investment opportunity
SHARING information	• A "sharing" presentation is meant to transfer knowledge • These presentations often provide project status updates, detail new trends, or outline new program details	• Outline new market trends and their potential impact on the company's business • Update team on business performance versus expectations

Next, identify who your audience is . . .

It is very difficult to sell your ideas if you don't know who your audience is

Don't be afraid to ask!

Ways to identify audience

- Ask whoever gave you the assignment who the primary decision makers are

- Ask a colleague who has worked on a similar presentation for details about the audience

- Ask for an old presentation or report on the project's topic to see who was included on the distribution list

. . . and think through the needs of your primary and secondary audiences to connect with their emotions

	Description	Questions to think through audience's needs
Primary audience	• People in the meeting you will be selling to or sharing ideas with most directly • Usually have a stake in the outcome of the project (e.g., affects their activities, budget, or performance)	• How do I think each primary audience member defines success for my project (and thus my presentation)? • What are the one to three things each member needs to hear to be persuaded to pursue my ideas?
Secondary audience	• Other audience members invited to your presentation meeting because of some indirect impact on their activities • Often have expertise in a particular aspect of your project	• How can these secondary audience members persuade the primary audience to pursue my ideas (i.e., give them an opportunity to defend my fact base)?

Consider sensitivities that often arise when there are multiple audience members

Sensitivity	What to consider		What you can do about it
Different levels of background	• Certain audience members may know every detail about your project and others know less or nothing at all		• Include some up-front context at the beginning of the presentation (either as speaking points or as a slide) to align everyone to the same starting point
Multiple functions present	• Meetings often include members from other functions and teams who may be interested in only one part of the presentation		• In the section relevant to their function or team, make sure to open the discussion to those persons to make them feel they can share their expertise
Varying interest in detail*	• Audience members always have different styles; some like to see all the details, and others do not		• Make sure to include some facts to back up your insights and recommendations • Can include additional supporting facts in the appendix to make the audience members feel confident that you have all the details
Conflicting opinions	• Two or more audience members have conflicting opinions about something in the project		• Interview audience members ahead of the meeting, time permitting, to understand their viewpoints and what they care most about • Use this information to try to resolve the conflicting opinions before the audience members disagree with each other during the meeting

* The next slide illustrates some of the varying levels of detail.

Varying levels of interest across audience affect how much detail to include on slides

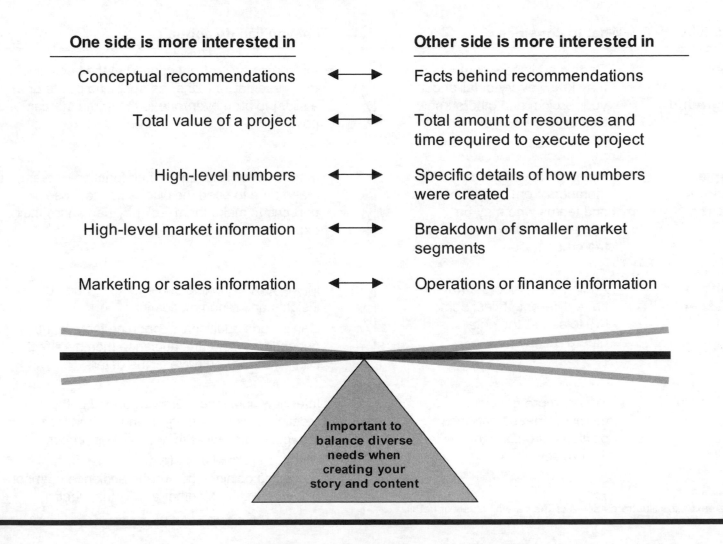

One side is more interested in		Other side is more interested in
Conceptual recommendations	⟷	Facts behind recommendations
Total value of a project	⟷	Total amount of resources and time required to execute project
High-level numbers	⟷	Specific details of how numbers were created
High-level market information	⟷	Breakdown of smaller market segments
Marketing or sales information	⟷	Operations or finance information

Important to balance diverse needs when creating your story and content

Balancing needs can help tailor presentations for different audiences and meeting time constraints

"Whether the audience is a handful of colleagues or clients at lunch or 10,000 convention-goers listening to a formal address, the secrets of a great story are largely the same."
Peter Gruber
HBR, December 2007*

Number of slides in presentation	Description	Example audience	Timing
1 slide	Concentrated summary of project's entire story in a single slide	Single manager	Short about 15 minutes
7-10 slides	Summary of project's story with a single slide backup for each primary point of story	Decision makers and select teammates	Medium about 30 minutes
30+ slides	Full debrief of project with multiple slides supporting each mini-story	Broader everyday team and/or partners	Long about 60+ minutes

* Peter Gruber, "The Four Truths of the Storyteller," *Harvard Business Review,* December 2007.

Next, "agendicize" the project before any information collection or analysis to guide your preparation

Definition of "agendicize"

Act of creating a list of research areas you want to investigate during a project based on your objective that will guide all your activities

Steps to "agendicize" the project

(1) Identify 3–6 areas of research that can be linked together to tell your story. Examples of areas include:
- Size of market
- Firm's position within market
- Competitor activities
- Opportunity areas
- Performance versus forecast
- Potential risks
- Customer relationships
- Partner relationships
- Benchmark comparisons
- Execution considerations

(2) For each research area, write down 1–4 research questions you want to answer

(3) For each question, identify and write down the data and analyses needed to answer it

Resulting benefits

1. Helps you think through what decision makers in the audience need to see to be persuaded to proceed with your ideas

2. Helps structure your thoughts at the very beginning of the project, allowing you to:
   - Remain focused on the end result (i.e., actionable recommendations)
   - Communicate your thought process to your manager early on by sharing the topics on paper (see next page for illustration)

PowerPoint Presentations That Sell

ILLUSTRATION: Create a one-page slide outlining project's topics (that you can review with your manager)

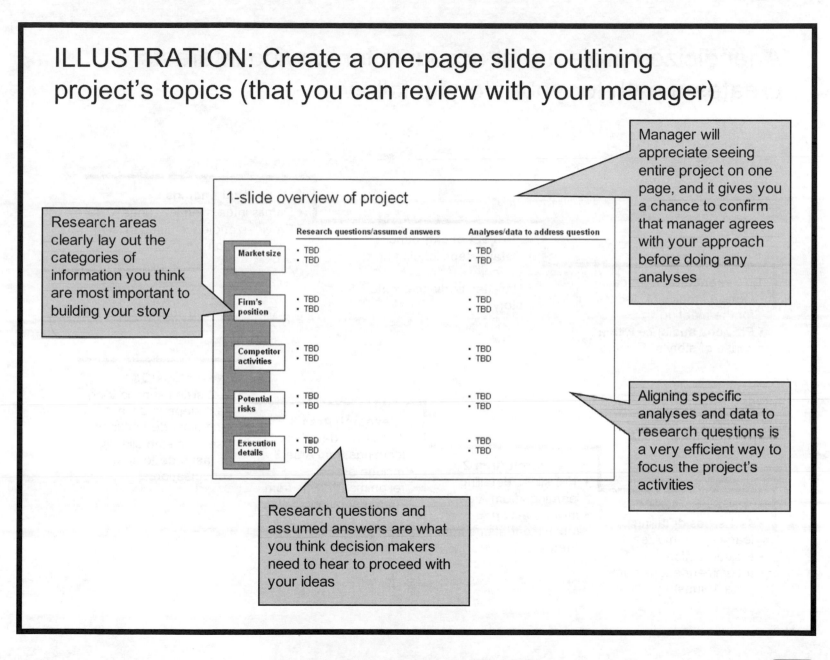

Agendicized project that accounts for varying interests creates a path for your story to follow

3. High-level findings
- Details interesting learnings
- Provides audience clues to story's outcome

2. Project background
- Details steps leading up to project
- Provides audience context for story

1. Presentation agenda
- Outlines topics of discussion for the meeting
- Provides audience with a sense of story's structure

7. Next steps/Q&A
- 1–2 slides summarizing next steps to drive recommended actions
- Use next step slide(s) as last slide to spark conversation

6. Research Area 3
- 1–4 slides detailing learnings from Area 3
- Include action recommendations from Area 3 substory

5. Research Area 2
- 1–4 slides detailing learnings from Area 2
- Include action recommendations from Area 2 substory

4. Research Area 1
- 1–4 slides detailing learnings from Area 1
- Include action recommendations from Area 1 substory

PowerPoint Presentations That Sell

At the beginning of the presentation, share the story's path with your audience by using an "agenda slide"

"Agenda slide" details

- 1-page slide that outlines the topics you plan to discuss during the meeting (the table of contents of your story's path)

- Agenda slide helps audience see your thought process and story structure up front before you jump to presentation

- Often, list of topics can help audience know when to ask particular questions (e.g., you're presenting Section 1, and a question comes up that is addressed in Section 2)

Place agenda slide right after title slide:

Topics to discuss today

1. Project context and background

2. Opportunity areas for our team (or business unit/company)

3. Competitor activity

4. Potential new business (or customer) to target

5. Risks to consider

6. Action plan and next steps

2

For longer presentations, the agenda slide can be used as a section divider throughout the presentation

When you have a long presentation (five or more slides per section), use the agenda page as a divider between sections to signal the start of the next part of your story and to give you and your audience a pause in the discussion

[Last page of Section 2]

10

Topics to discuss today

1. Project context and background
2. Opportunity areas for our team (or business unit/company)
3. **Competitor activity**
4. Potential new business (or customer) to target
5. Risks to consider
6. Action plan and next steps

11

[First page of Section 3]

12

Notes

- To make it clear which section is about to begin, bold the text and put a rectangle* around the text (can make other topics a gray color)
- Try to use divider page only for longer presentations (five or more slides per section)

* See Chapter 10, "Quick Hit FAQs" in Part III for more details on creating a rectangle.

Chapter 4 Outline Your Presentation through Storyboarding

Simple techniques to plan, design, and deliver presentations that get results

Another technique introduced to help you use a story-telling mindset is storyboarding slides before going to the computer. Storyboards are handwritten visual illustrations of what your story's path could look like in PowerPoint. Creating a storyboard allows you to translate your agendicized thoughts into handwritten slides. Although completing this means you have to invest some time up front, thinking through how you want to present your content saves a lot of time in the long run. It is always easier to edit than to create, and if you visualize your story presentation from the beginning, it is easier to modify and adjust as you move through your research. If part of the story seems awkward or out of place, this is the time to eliminate or modify the information to prevent you from completing too much research on a noncritical topic. Storyboarding can save you from spending time collecting information that will not make it into the final presentation. Although a presentation is a working document and it is not always possible to know the entire story at the beginning, being mindful of this storytelling mindset and taking it one step further to storyboard your slides can help you remain focused on the most important information to collect, ultimately making you more efficient.

What's next: Storyboarding

What's next

Create handwritten storyboards
- Storyboards are handwritten visual illustrations of what your story's path could look like in PowerPoint
- Use the following pages to illustrate what your findings could look like as a set of slides *before doing any analysis*

What you've done

You have used a storytelling mindset to create an agendicized path for your story and addressed audience's varying needs

Craft mini-stories on each slide
- A mini-story is an individual message or insight that you want to tell your audience on each slide of the presentation
- Linking these mini-stories together creates a cohesive story that consists of actionable recommendations

Use storyboards to translate your agendicized thoughts into handwritten slides

Great storytellers use storyboard technique	Helps visualize findings of analyses on final slides	More efficient use of time

- Storyboard is a *handwritten* piece of paper that outlines each slide in the presentation

- Great storytellers (movie/TV directors, advertisers, writers) all use storyboards to outline their vision before using a camera or computer

- "Rough sketches" go a long way to help you organize your thoughts and focus on the most important analyses

- Use an entire sheet to make sketch or divide a sheet into four quadrants to sketch four slides on same sheet:

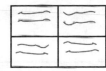

- After creating a handwritten grid on paper, write down the slide title and one or two key learnings* on the right-hand side of each slide to see the story develop *before working in PowerPoint*

- Even though handwritten storyboarding takes time, thinking through how you want to present your content at the beginning of project saves a lot of time in the long run

- Practicing this technique at the onset of a project is the best way to make stronger presentations and differentiate yourself

* Key learnings highlight the most important insights from the slide's content; more detail is provided in Part II.

ILLUSTRATION: Example storyboard from Part I*

Example storyboard for pages in Part I*

Including at least some content under each part of the slide can be helpful as a guide (may change once you go to PowerPoint)

Writing out titles on each slide helps you outline the story before doing any analysis

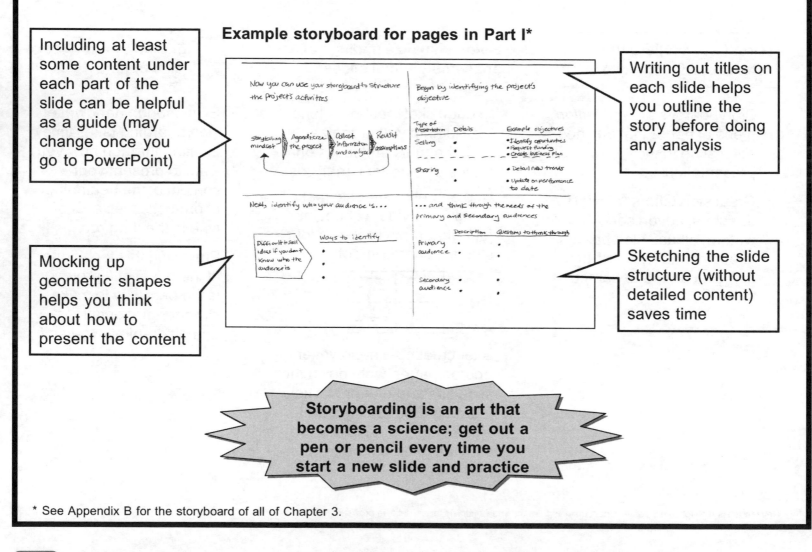

Mocking up geometric shapes helps you think about how to present the content

Sketching the slide structure (without detailed content) saves time

Storyboarding is an art that becomes a science; get out a pen or pencil every time you start a new slide and practice

* See Appendix B for the storyboard of all of Chapter 3.

Think of your presentation as a collection of mini-stories on each slide

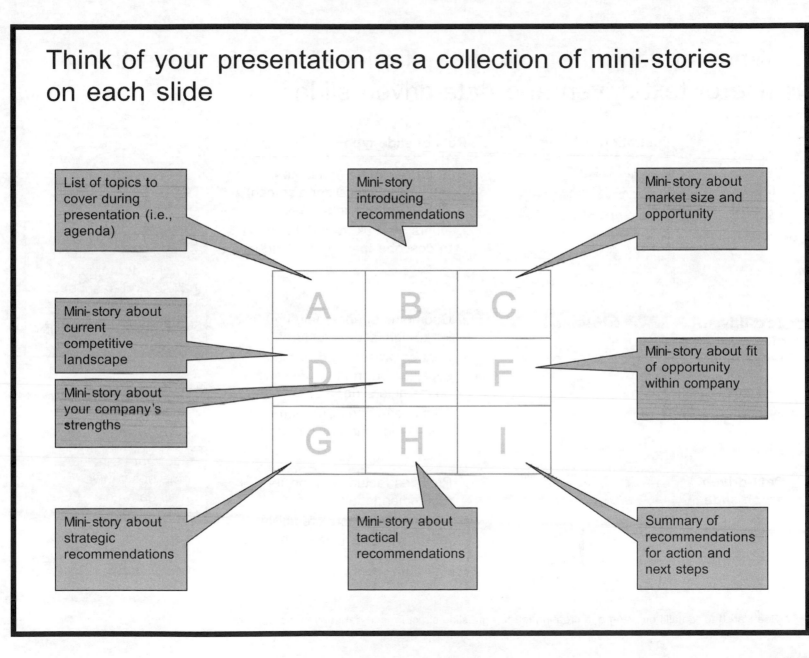

When crafting the collection of mini-stories, balance the use of text-driven and data-driven slides

	Illustration	**Role of slide type**

Text-driven slide (basic)*

Example Basic Text-Driven Slide

Heading (primary)		Heading (secondary)	
Category A	• Example details 1 • Example details 2	• Example supporting details 1 • Example supporting details 2	
Category B	• Example details 1 • Example details 2	• Example supporting details 1 • Example supporting details 2	
Category C	• Example details 1 • Example details 2	• Example supporting details 1 • Example supporting details 2	

Source: TBD

- Allows for more conceptual discussion topics but also can include data points
- Offers a break from data charts to describe the situation further

> Text-driven slides should be formatted left to right (do not just use bullets and dashes) to take the audience through the story more efficiently*

Text-driven slide (advanced)*

Example Advanced Text-Driven Slide

Heading 1	Heading 2
• Example information • Example information • Example information	• Example information • Example information • Example information

Source: TBD

- Geometric shapes help create left-to-right slide structure*
- Shapes present two or more separate but related messages on a single slide
- Advanced charts are more interesting than basic ones

Data-driven graph slide*

Example Data-Driven Slide

Graph title
Units of measure

Series A	100
Series B	75
Series C	50
Series D	25

Key learnings
- Detailed insight 1 with supporting information
- Detailed insight 2 with supporting information

Source: TBD

- Provides factual support for recommendations
- Gives project more credibility (assuming data is relevant)

> Important to include some descriptive text on all data chart slides to call attention to the most important information

* See Part II for details on using and creating left-to-right slide structure and data-driven graph slides.

PowerPoint Presentations That Sell

To deliver consistent, action-oriented slides, consider four steps while drawing the storyboard

Steps to consider

1. Slide message
What message or mini-story am I trying to convey on this slide?

2. Action-oriented
Does my slide message lead to action? If not, what additional information is needed?

3. Effective communication
Does my slide structure effectively communicate my message? If not, what other geometric shapes (see pages 61–62 for more details) could improve the communication?

4. Necessary information
Are all the data points on the slide necessary to defend my recommendations? If not, delete unnecessary information

Rationale for approach

- Ensures that slide's message is relevant to audience and action-oriented

- Forces you to prioritize the most important information to present

- Provokes better conversation during the presentation rather than at the end of the meeting

EXERCISE: Try drawing a storyboard!

Think about the last project you worked on or the last presentation you created. Focus on just one of the sections of that presentation and draw a very basic storyboard by using the following steps:

1. Take a blank piece of paper and draw a horizontal line and a vertical line through the middle to create a grid with four boxes (see image below)
2. Think about four brief sentences that tell the story of the section you selected
3. Starting in the top left box, write with pencil or pen the first sentence that begins your story. Then write the remaining sentences in the other three boxes
4. Congratulations—you've created your first storyboard!

Example

Our main 3 competitors are starting to target new customers.	Our market share is declining as a result.
①	②
These customers are telling us we need to improve.	An opportunity exists to address this threat.
③	④

Go to the next page to add more detail to your storyboard

PowerPoint Presentations That Sell

EXERCISE: Draw a more detailed storyboard with mini-stories

Now, for a project you're currently working on, draw a four-page storyboard with sentence headers and one or two pieces of information you want to include on each slide:

1. Handwrite four sentences with a pencil or pen at the top of each box

2. Think through the content you want to put on each slide (your mini-story) and decide how to structure the thoughts (Part II will provide more guidance on structuring a slide's content)

3. Handwrite your ideas within each box to give you a starting point before you approach the computer

Example (continued from previous page)

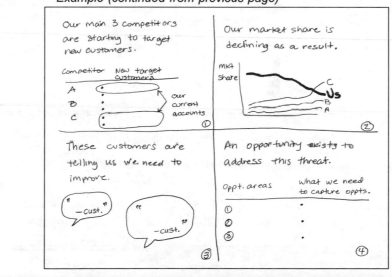

Keep in mind that the handwritten storyboard will evolve as you translate it into PowerPoint

Project onset → **Project completion**

- Collect data and conduct analyses
- Transfer storyboard into actual slides

- Iterate presentation of data until the vital information is highlighted
- Review hard copy of presentation draft; this often leads to additional edits
- Fine-tune key learnings to align with important data

- As project progresses, new analyses will be necessary
- Storyboard these analyses first, then conduct analyses, and then transfer to PowerPoint

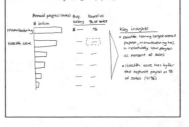

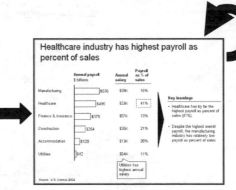

Summary of project/analysis timeline

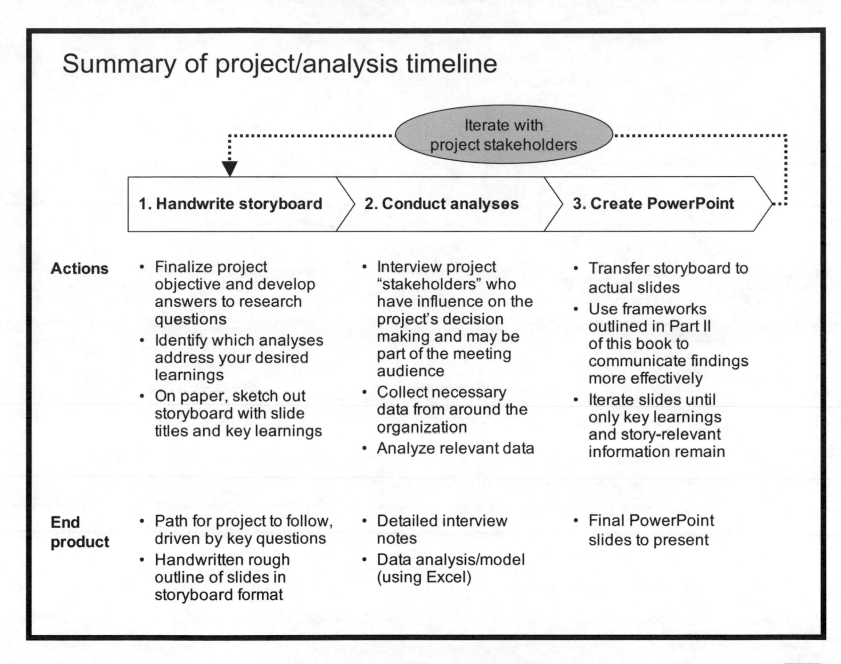

Iterate with project stakeholders

	1. Handwrite storyboard	2. Conduct analyses	3. Create PowerPoint
Actions	• Finalize project objective and develop answers to research questions • Identify which analyses address your desired learnings • On paper, sketch out storyboard with slide titles and key learnings	• Interview project "stakeholders" who have influence on the project's decision making and may be part of the meeting audience • Collect necessary data from around the organization • Analyze relevant data	• Transfer storyboard to actual slides • Use frameworks outlined in Part II of this book to communicate findings more effectively • Iterate slides until only key learnings and story-relevant information remain
End product	• Path for project to follow, driven by key questions • Handwritten rough outline of slides in storyboard format	• Detailed interview notes • Data analysis/model (using Excel)	• Final PowerPoint slides to present

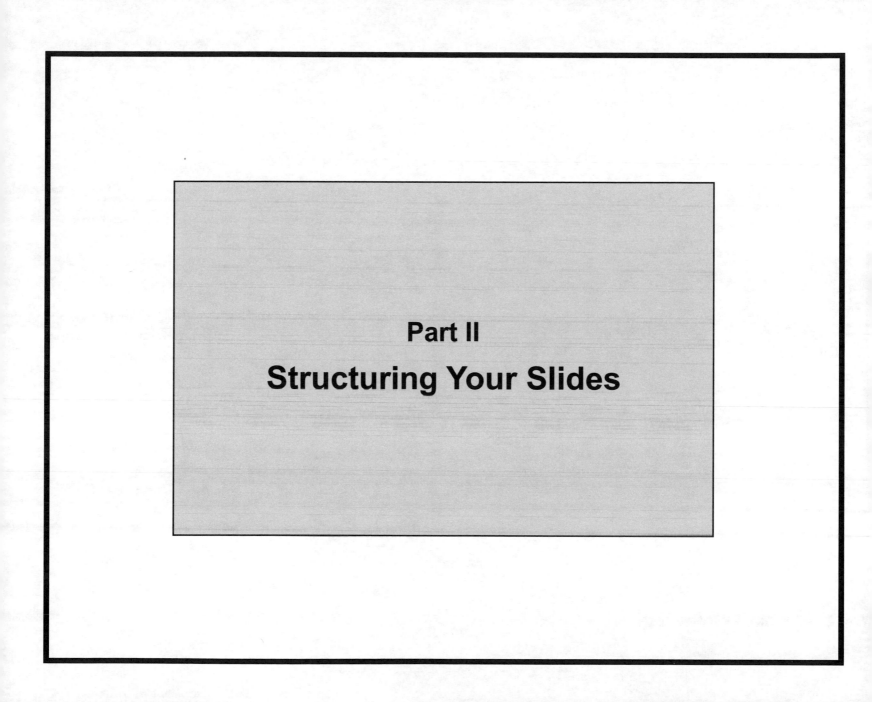

Chapter 5 Smart Slide Structure Techniques: Think Left to Right

Simple techniques to plan, design, and deliver presentations that get results

Part II focuses on structuring a slide's content. This is often an area professionals struggle with: "I know what I want to say, but how should I say it?" This part provides simple techniques to structure your slides to design and deliver presentations that get results. For example, one technique is to consider structuring a slide's content from left to right (rather than from top to bottom with bullets and dashes). This is the way people commonly read, and it makes the content more easily digestible for the audience. A left-to-right format can engage readers more easily because it serves as a natural guiding hand as you take readers from point A to point B. It also can allow you to fit more information on a slide while making it actually look less cluttered.

The main goal of Chapter 5 is to move you away from using only the top-to-bottom long list of bullets and dashes that we all use *way too often*. Chapter 5 takes you through the steps of how to start thinking from left to right, and then Part III details how to create the shapes and text boxes necessary to use the left-to-right structure. Don't be discouraged if you think the examples in this chapter look too complicated to create on your own. Chapter 10 in Part III has simple step-by-step instructions with illustrations to create these shapes and text boxes.

Use "smart slide structure" to engage the audience: Tell your story from left to right* across the slide . . .

Rationale for telling stories from left to right

- The left-to-right format is how people think and read

- Makes the slide's content more easily readable for audience

- Can use "categories," "headings," and shapes to divide content on page, allowing audience to focus on particular pieces of the story

This slide structure takes practice; be patient and use the following pages to create your own slides in a left-to-right format

*Rather than the top-to-bottom format with bullets and dashes.

PowerPoint Presentations That Sell

. . . Rather than using the top-to-bottom bullet and dash format to tell a story

Challenges of using top-to-bottom structure

Lack of flow	• Top-to-bottom bulleted structure does not show the flow of a story • First-level bullets sometimes are linked together and follow one another sequentially, but it is hard for the audience to digest each piece of the story when the bullets are on top of one another • If first-level bullets are *not* directly related to one another, it is confusing for the audience to see them in one long vertical list • Secondary- and tertiary-level bullets often detail similar things across each set of bullets, but it is difficult for the audience to make comparisons
Confusing style	• Bulleted items listed closer to the bottom of the list can be perceived as less important • Smaller font size of lower-level bullets is often hard to read and suggests the information is less important

Less efficient structure (top-to-bottom)

> Benefits, both visual and verbal, created by using left-to-right structure
>
> • **Breaks up monotony of slide after slide of bullets and dashes**
>   – Each slide has its own story, as discussed in Part I, but using the same top-to-bottom, bullet-dash structure does not allow stories to be visually unique
> • **Quickly shows audience how you think about content's structure**
>   – Structure is a helpful tool to tell your story
>   – Structure on a slide can influence the audience's perception of how well you understand the topic, which is a positive reflection on you
> • **Helps you verbally lay out the way the content will be discussed**
>   – When presenting, you can summarize the categories of information rather than going right into the first set of bullets
>   – This is a helpful approach to get the audience excited to hear more
> • **Allows focus on a particular area of interest on the slide**
>   – Some audience members are interested in only particular sections of the content (e.g., on this slide, just the "Benefit" topic and not "Supporting rationale")
>   – Category-topic structure divides the content to allow these audience members to focus on information of interest
>   – Similarly, you can draw audience's attention more easily to a specific category or topic when a question arises
> • **Using left-to-right structure helps you present your content more effectively and differentiates you in meetings**

First step in creating a left-to-right structure is to think of the slide as having two sides

Left side   *Right side*

Think of the slide as being split into two minislides—one on the left and one on the right

- Left side of slide is the content that introduces the slide's story
- Right side of slide is content that concludes story

This technique allows the audience to digest the first part of the story (the left side) without feeling obligated to keep reading downward

Next step is identifying "categories" and "topics" of information covered in your content

Steps to convert to left to right	Details
Find 2–4 "categories" of information	• A category is usually a common theme that captures what the first-level bullet is discussing • Categories usually come from the first-level bullets in the original top-to-bottom list (you may identify one category per first-level bullet) • The category name should be a short phrase
Find about 2 common topics discussed *WITHIN* each category	• Even though you have a long list of items across multiple bullets, you should be able to identify common topics being discussed within each set of bullets • Topics are themes that usually are detailed in secondary- and tertiary-level bullets • The topic name should be just a few words • Common examples of topic names are "Recommendation," "Examples," "Pros/Cons," "Details," "Supporting Evidence," "Rationale"
Put details of content into category-topic structure	• Once the structure is created, display the content within the corresponding category and topic • Detailed content should be displayed as bulleted text boxes (see later in this chapter and Chapter 10, "Quick Hit FAQs," for more details on creating bulleted text boxes)

Now think of your slide as a grid to help create the visual layout for a category-topic structure

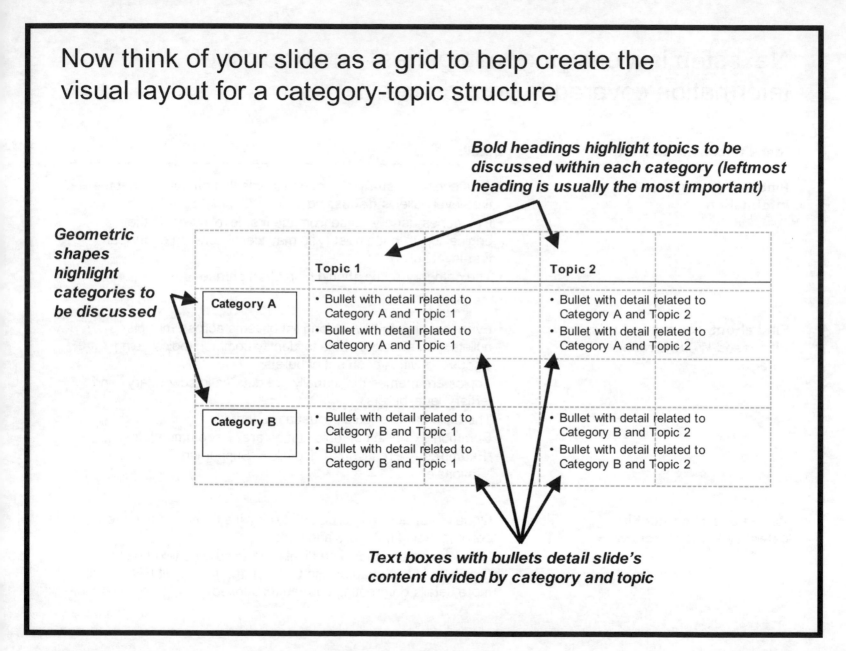

Benefits, both visual and verbal, created by using left-to-right structure

Benefit	Supporting rationale
Breaks up monotony of slide after slide of bullets and dashes	• Each slide has its own story, as discussed in Part I, but using the same top-to-bottom, bullet-dash structure does not allow stories to be visually unique
Quickly shows audience how you think about content's structure	• Structure is a helpful tool to tell your story • Structure on a slide can influence the audience's perception of how well you understand the topic, which is a positive reflection on you
Helps you verbally lay out how content will be discussed	• When presenting, you can summarize the categories of information rather than going right into the first set of bullets • This is a helpful approach to get the audience excited to hear more
Allows focus on a particular area of interest on the slide	• Some audience members are interested in only particular sections of content (e.g., on this slide, just the "Benefit" topic and not "Supporting rationale") • Category-topic structure separates the content to allow these audience members to focus on information of interest • Similarly, you can draw the audience's attention more easily to a specific category or topic when a question arises

Using left-to-right structure helps you present your content more effectively and differentiates you in meetings

ILLUSTRATION: Comparing left-to-right and top-to-bottom formats

Less efficient (top-to-bottom)

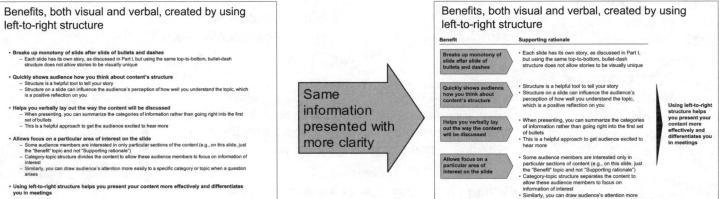

More efficient (left-to-right)

Same information presented with more clarity

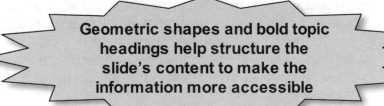

Geometric shapes and bold topic headings help structure the slide's content to make the information more accessible

Within the grid, use geometric shapes to *structure* the slide's information . . .

Structuring shape	Illustration in slide	Purpose	How to create
Category box	Category A • Detail 1 • Detail 2 / Category B • Detail 1 • Detail 2	• Category boxes draw attention to themes being discussed on the slide • Bulleted comments detail the category's points of interest	Click on the AutoShapes icon in the Draw menu bar* and click on "Rectangle" in "Basic Shapes"
Separating Line	Heading • Detail 1 • Detail 2	• Line separates headings from detailed content (more visually pleasing than underlining actual text)	Click on the AutoShapes icon and click on "Lines" (see Part III for more details)
Flow arrow	Topic 1 > Topic 2 • Detail 1 • Detail 1 • Detail 2 • Detail 2	• Flow arrows illustrate progression from one topic to another • Bulleted comments detail the topic's points of interest	Click on the AutoShapes icon and click on "Pentagon" in "Block Arrows"
Triangle/ diamond	Detail / Text / Detail Detail	• Triangle (or diamond) describes three (or four) key topics	Click on the AutoShapes icon and click on "Isosceles Triangle" in "Basic Shapes"

*Find the "Draw" menu by going to "View" → "Toolbars" → "Drawing" (menu should show up along bottom of screen).

. . . and to *emphasize* slide's information

Emphasizing shape	Illustration	Purpose	How to create
Learnings arrow	Supporting info ▶ Learnings	• Acts as a divider for slide's content • Big arrow draws attention to "key learnings"	Click on the AutoShapes icon* and click on "Isosceles Triangle" in "Basic Shapes"; rotate by using Rotate and Flip buttons in Draw menu
Shadowed box	Learnings •Insight 1 •Insight 2	• Shadowed box frames the "key learnings" on the slide	Click on "Rectangle" in "Basic Shapes"; use "Shadow Style" in Draw menu*
Starburst	Key insight	• Starburst highlights a key insight and is eye-catching	Click on "16-Point Star" in "Stars and Banners" within AutoShapes*
Callout box	Callout to add insight from data	• Use callout boxes to add commentary to data slide	Click on "Rectangular Callout" in "Callouts" within AutoShapes*

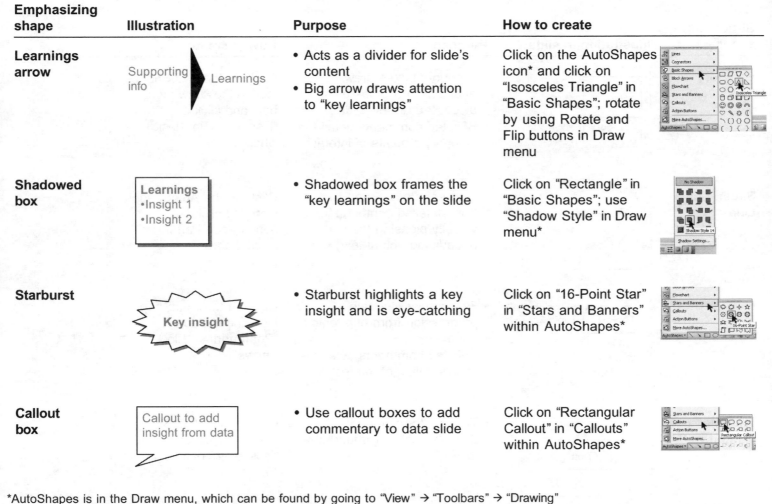

*AutoShapes is in the Draw menu, which can be found by going to "View" → "Toolbars" → "Drawing" (menu should show up along bottom of screen).

PowerPoint Presentations That Sell

Once structure is created, use text boxes to structure and communicate the content

Text box type	Illustration	Purpose	How to create
Bold heading	**Heading** • Detail 1 • Detail 2	• Draws audience's attention to topics that will be discussed • Note: use line tool (see Part III) rather than underline font style	Use Chapter 10, "Quick Hit FAQs," in Part III to see step-by-step instructions for creating text boxes, changing font styling, and adding bullets
Text box (nonbullet)	Heading • Detail 1 • Detail 2 Insights or summary	• Communicates slide's content	
Bulleted text box	Heading • Detail 1 • Detail 2	• Communicates slide's content in easy-to-read format • Bullets are more efficient in expressing ideas than is basic text in paragraph format	

Next, use font styling, coloring, shading, and graphics to draw the audience's attention to story-vital information

	Examples*	**But be careful . . .**
Font styling	• **Bold key phrases/headings** • *Italicize key phrases* • <u>Underline key phrases</u> • CAPITALIZE KEY PHRASES	• Style only short phrases (1–4 words) within a longer string of words or effect gets lost • Try to avoid using different font sizes on a single slide—can be distracting
Coloring	• **Blue key phrase** • **Red key phrase** • **Green key phrase**	• Avoid light colors such as yellow, because they may not show up clearly on screen or printouts • Too many colors on one slide can be distracting; alter color of vital information only
Shading and outlining	• Key data point or learning* • Key data point or learning*	• Only shade or outline key pieces of information—too much shading will diminish the impact
Graphics and images	• Use images (of product, Web site, process flow, etc.) to relate text with visual graphics • "Print Screen" (Fn+Prnt Scrn) will capture an image on the screen to paste into the slide	• Include text next to images to call out important content • Graphic images increase the size of the file, making it more difficult to e-mail

*See "Chapter 10, Quick Hit FAQs," for step-by-step instructions for styling font, creating rectangles, and pasting images.

Another way to focus only on story-vital information is to remove unnecessary text

A few things to remember when using bulleted text

- Use phrases in presentations rather than complete sentences

- Rely on your speaking points to expand on phrases

- Try to keep each bullet to two or three lines when possible

- Fewer words are better—makes it easier for audience to read ("the" often can be deleted)

Questions to ask yourself when looking at text on a slide

- What is the main point I'm trying to make with each bullet?

- Is each word necessary to make that point?

- If I wanted to cut a third of the words, which would I cut?

ILLUSTRATION: Cut unneeded text

Less efficient (too much text)

- The Olympic Games is an international multisport event established for both summer and winter games.

- There have been two generations of the Olympic Games; the first were the Ancient Olympic Games held at Olympia, Greece. The second, known as the Modern Olympic Movement, were first held in 1896, in Athens, Greece.

- The IOC has become the governing body of the "Olympic Movement," a conglomeration of sporting federations that are responsible for the organization of the Games.

Cut unneeded text

- ~~The~~ Olympic Games is an international multisport event ~~established~~ for both summer and winter games.

- ~~There have been~~ two generations ~~of the Olympic~~ Games; ~~the first were the~~ Ancient Olympic Games held at Olympia, Greece. ~~The second, known as the~~ Modern Olympic Movement, ~~were first held~~ in 1896, in Athens, Greece.

- ~~The~~ IOC ~~has become the~~ govern~~ing body of~~ the "Olympic Movement," a conglomeration sporting federations ~~that are responsible for the organization of the Games~~.

Improved text with more white space

- Olympic Games is an international multisport event for both summer and winter

- Two generations of Games:
  - Ancient Olympic Games held at Olympia, Greece
  - Modern Olympic Movement started in 1896 in Athens, Greece

- IOC governs the "Olympic Movement," a conglomeration of sporting federations

Source: Text is adapted from Wikipedia article "Olympics."

Exercise: Now try cutting unneeded text!

Find a slide you created recently that has a set of bullets with a lot of text (four or more lines) and try to eliminate unneeded text by recalling the key questions:

1. What is the main point I'm trying to make with each bullet?
2. Is each word necessary to make that point?
3. If I wanted to cut half the words, which ones would I cut?

Less efficient (too much text)

- ~~The~~ Olympic Games is an international multisport event ~~established~~ for both summer and winter games.
- ~~There have been~~ two generations ~~of the Olympic~~ Games; ~~the first were the~~ Ancient Olympic Games held at Olympia, Greece. ~~The second, known as the~~ Modern Olympic Movement, ~~were first held~~ in 1896, in Athens, Greece.
- ~~The~~ IOC ~~has become the~~ governing ~~body~~ of the "Olympic Movement," a conglomeration of sporting federations ~~that are responsible for the organization of the Games.~~

Same story but with more clarity

More efficient (less text, more white space)

- Olympic Games is an international multisport event for both summer and winter
- Two generations of Games:
  - Ancient Olympic Games held at Olympia, Greece
  - Modern Olympic Movement started in 1896 in Athens, Greece
- IOC governs the "Olympic Movement," a conglomeration of sporting federations

Also, left and top alignment* is important for creating the left-to-right slide structure

Recommendation	Rationale	Illustration	
		What NOT to do	**What to do***
Left align headings with corresponding text boxes* (instead of center alignment)	• Left alignment encourages audience to follow the content across the page • Center alignment can make it difficult to see which heading is connected with which content text box • Note: also left align slide title	Heading 1 •Detail 1 with support •Detail 2 with support •Detail 3 with support •Detail 4 with support	Heading 1 •Detail 1 with support •Detail 2 with support •Detail 3 with support •Detail 4 with support
Left and top align text within geometric shapes* (instead of center/middle alignment)	• Left alignment encourages audience to follow the content across the page • Better for shapes and text boxes to have same alignment	Category box •Detail 1 •Detail 2 •Detail 3 •Detail 4	Category box •Detail 1 •Detail 2 •Detail 3 •Detail 4
Top align shapes with corresponding text boxes* (instead of middle alignment)	• Top alignment creates cleaner look • Middle alignment can make it difficult to see which heading is connected with which content text box	•Detail 1 Category box •Detail 2 •Detail 3 •Detail 4	Category box •Detail 1 •Detail 2 •Detail 3 •Detail 4

*See Chapter 10, "Quick Hit FAQs," for step-by-step instructions for aligning text boxes.

PowerPoint Presentations That Sell

ILLUSTRATION: Creating left-to-right slide (from p. 5)

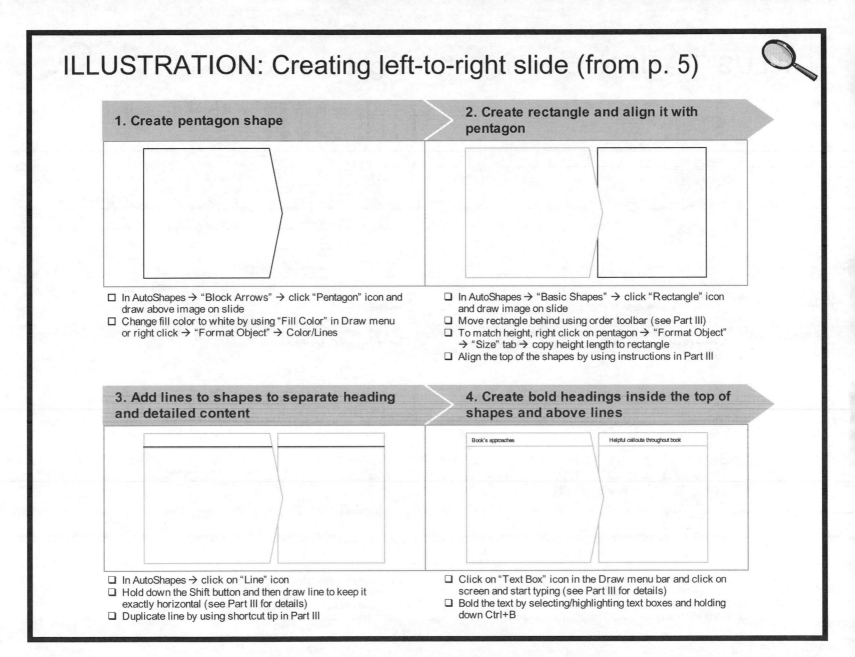

1. Create pentagon shape

- ❑ In AutoShapes → "Block Arrows" → click "Pentagon" icon and draw above image on slide
- ❑ Change fill color to white by using "Fill Color" in Draw menu or right click → "Format Object" → Color/Lines

2. Create rectangle and align it with pentagon

- ❑ In AutoShapes → "Basic Shapes" → click "Rectangle" icon and draw image on slide
- ❑ Move rectangle behind using order toolbar (see Part III)
- ❑ To match height, right click on pentagon → "Format Object" → "Size" tab → copy height length to rectangle
- ❑ Align the top of the shapes by using instructions in Part III

3. Add lines to shapes to separate heading and detailed content

- ❑ In AutoShapes → click on "Line" icon
- ❑ Hold down the Shift button and then draw line to keep it exactly horizontal (see Part III for details)
- ❑ Duplicate line by using shortcut tip in Part III

4. Create bold headings inside the top of shapes and above lines

Book's approaches   Helpful callouts throughout book

- ❑ Click on "Text Box" icon in the Draw menu bar and click on screen and start typing (see Part III for details)
- ❑ Bold the text by selecting/highlighting text boxes and holding down Ctrl+B

5. Add category boxes

- ❑ In AutoShapes → "Basic Shapes" → click "Rectangle" icon and draw image on slide
- ❑ To add text, click on shape and start typing
- ❑ To wrap and top align text within shape, right click → "Format Object" → look at "Text Box" tab (see Part III)
- ❑ Change fill color by using "Fill Color" in Draw menu

6. Add bulleted text box with detailed content

- ❑ Click on "Text Box" icon in Draw menu → click on screen and type
- ❑ To add bullets, highlight text within text box and click "Bullets" icon under "Format" menu (for more details on bullet alignment, see Part III)

7. Add geometric shapes (star and arrow in this example)

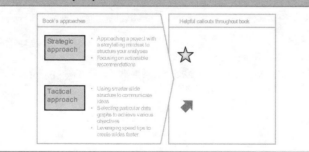

- ❑ In AutoShapes → "Stars" and "Block Arrows" → click "5-Point Star" and "Right Arrow" and draw images
- ❑ Change fill colors by using "Fill Color" button
- ❑ Rotate by clicking on object and using green circle

8. Add basic text box with more detailed content

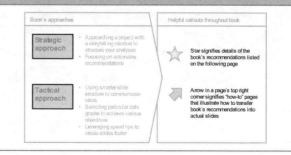

- ❑ Click on "Text Box" icon in the Draw menu bar → click on screen and type
- ❑ Duplicate text box and drag it down while maintaining left alignment by using shortcut tip in Part III

EXERCISE: Now you try it!

Find a slide you created recently that looks like the top-to-bottom slide below on the left and convert it to the slide below on the right in the left-to-right format by using the following steps:

1. Handwrite a one-page storyboard of a left-to-right slide based on the content in your original slide

2. Create actual slide by using geometric shapes, text boxes, and other tools from the "Draw" menu, as detailed previously and in Part III

3. For additional tips on how to create slides quickly, see Part III

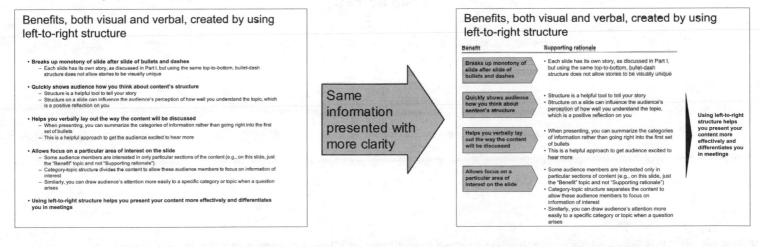

Less efficient (top-to-bottom)

More efficient (left-to-right)

Same information presented with more clarity

Keep in mind that a single piece of information on a slide can be sufficient (and just as impactful)*

It's okay to include just one piece of information on the slide to get your point across

*Don't be afraid to leave white space (space that does not have any text or objects) on the page.

PowerPoint Presentations That Sell

Chapter 6 Selecting the Right Data Graphs

Simple techniques to plan, design, and deliver presentations that get results

The second half of Part II addresses one of the most common struggles in preparing a presentation: how to select and create compelling charts that use data. The first thing to remember about presenting data is that you should seek to answer your audience's questions on data slides before the audience has a chance to ask them. In other words, the audience should not have to guess what information is on a certain slide or make their own calculations; this should be done for them by creating clear slides that articulate calculations and sources of information. A three-step technique is introduced in Chapter 6 to help you do this: introducing, revealing, and supporting your story. This section explains how a slide title can be used to introduce a story, saving space for the data you plan to present on the actual slide and providing insight into why this slide is important to the audience. It can also help to pique the audience's interest in the information about to be shared. This section also outlines the most effective way to structure and format a slide when you are revealing key learnings as well as maximize the impact of presenting data to support your story.

What's next: Improving data-driven slides

What's next

Address audience questions by using three slide elements

- Consider the questions an audience member is thinking about when looking at a data slide
- Slide title, key learnings, and supporting data introduce, reveal, and support the slide's story

What you've done

You have learned how to use left-to-right slide structure to organize your actionable insights in a storytelling format

Selectively choose how to present data

- Data-driven slides are very influential—impact can be diminished if the information is not presented clearly
- Select particular data graphs on the basis of the message you're trying to deliver

PowerPoint Presentations That Sell

Answer audience members' questions on data slides before they have a chance to ask them

Questions the audience thinks about on a data slide
Next set of slides addresses how to answer them

High-level

1. What are the insights from the data that I care about?

2. Which key data point(s) should I be looking at on the slide?

Detailed

3. What data am I looking at (e.g., data graph title/description and units)?

4. In a large set of data, which data series is the biggest and which is the smallest?

5. How much have the numbers in the chart changed over time (i.e., percentage change year over year) or compared to something else?

Don't make audience members guess about what the information is or make their own calculations

Use three slide elements to address audience questions by introducing, revealing, and supporting your story

1. Slide title *(introduce story)*

- Slide title introduces mini-story and gets audience excited about reading the rest of the slide
- Provides specific insight into the situation that is displayed on rest of the slide

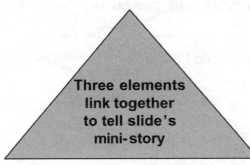

Three elements link together to tell slide's mini-story

2. Learnings/recommendations *(reveal story)*

- Reveal your interesting learnings directly on the slide rather than just as talking points
- Learnings should not just repeat data already on the slide
- Right side of slide is a good place to display learnings

3. Supporting data analysis *(support story)*

- Data drives the insights that lead to actionable recommendations
- Data provides assurance to the audience that the recommendations have factual support
- See end of Part II for details on how to maximize the impact of presenting data

PowerPoint Presentations That Sell

Make the slide title meaningful and pique the audience's interest in your story

- Think of your title as the audience's first impression of a slide (remember, you get only one chance to make a first impression!)
- Try to avoid generic titles because that wastes valuable "real estate" on the slide and the title is your chance to introduce the story before the audience reads the rest of the content

Generic title *(less effective)*	Meaningful title *(more effective)*
Product Advantages	Product Advantages Cross Multiple Aspects of Your Business
Business Unit A's Market Share	Business Unit A's Market Share Has Declined to the Benefit of Competitor Z
Sales and Profit Growth	Despite Slow Sales Growth, Profit Growth Has Exceeded Expectations
Budget versus Actual	Actual Costs Stayed within Budget

Key learnings (plus title) should be enough to tell the *entire* story to the audience

SAMPLE SLIDE

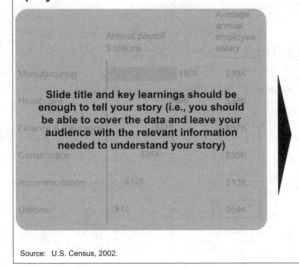

Manufacturing industry has highest annual payroll

Slide title and key learnings should be enough to tell your story (i.e., you should be able to cover the data and leave your audience with the relevant information needed to understand your story)

Key learnings

- Despite the highest overall payroll, the manufacturing industry does not have the highest average salary

- Utilities industry averages highest average salary ($64K per year) despite having lowest overall annual payroll

Source: U.S. Census, 2002.

Considerations

- Learnings tell audience members what they need to know—interesting insights and action items from the slide's mini-story

- You should be able to cover the data on the slide and leave the audience with sufficient information

- Use short, bulleted phrases (three lines or less if space allows)

- See Chapter 10, "Quick Hit FAQs," for instructions for creating bold headings and bulleted text box

Questions to ask yourself when creating "learnings"

1. Is this just a summary of the data on the slide or is it insightful and/or actionable? **If just a summary, delete from learnings section**

2. Does this bullet point fill in a missing piece of my story? **If no, delete**

3. Will this information change a decision maker's viewpoint or further defend my position? **If no, delete or consider rephrasing**

Next, identify the message you want to deliver before choosing which data graph to use

Message type	Example messages
Comparison I want to compare two or more things	• Unit A has higher sales than Unit B • Profit margin of Product W is larger than that of Products X, Y, and Z • Category U no longer has the highest costs compared with other categories
Distribution I want to show how something breaks down into smaller pieces	• Companies A, B, and C make up 80% of the market's sales • R&D spending as percentage of sales varies widely across the industry, but growth in spending is fairly constant from year to year
Track over time I want to show a change in something over time	• Company X's stock price has been consistently above the overall stock market • There have been large fluctuations in market shares over a 12-month period

Identifying the message will help you choose which graph to use to present your data

Now select data graph on the basis of your message*

Message type	Basic graphs to select for a single data series	Layering multiple data series on same graph type

Comparison
I want to compare two or more things

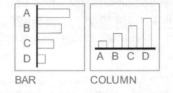

BAR   COLUMN

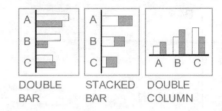

DOUBLE BAR   STACKED BAR   DOUBLE COLUMN

Distribution
I want to show how something breaks down into smaller pieces

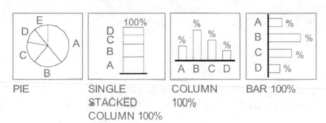

PIE   SINGLE STACKED COLUMN 100%   COLUMN 100%   BAR 100%

REFLECTION BAR 100%

Track over time
I want to show a change in something over time

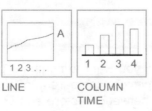

LINE   COLUMN TIME

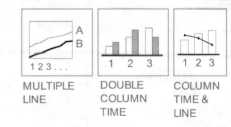

MULTIPLE LINE   DOUBLE COLUMN TIME   COLUMN TIME & LINE

*Rationale for selecting specific graphs across the message types is detailed on the following three pages.

Comparison messages: rationale for selecting one graph versus another

Comparison graph	Rationale for selecting particular graph
BAR	• Bar comparison graphs are especially useful when you have 4–8 groups and the order of the groups is most important to your message • Quickly illustrates the relative difference between groups when ordered by size • Easier to layer on more data series by using text boxes to the right (see pp. 87–88)
COLUMN	• Column comparison graphs can be helpful when comparing only a few groups (2–4) or many groups (more than 8) • More difficult to layer additional data series on column graphs
DOUBLE BAR / **DOUBLE COLUMN**	• Double graphs are useful when you want to compare two series of data (e.g., two years of data, two business units) across multiple groups on the same graph • Do not use double graphs with more than five groups—looks too cluttered • Double bar makes it easier to layer on more data series by using text boxes to the right versus double column (see p. 87 for illustration)
STACKED BAR	• Stacked bars are useful when you want to compare groups of something that can be broken down into smaller pieces (compare total sales across retailers but also how those sales break down between in-store and online) • There are usually two messages being told: (1) order of overall data (length of total bar) and (2) differences in the composition of overall data between groups

PowerPoint Presentations That Sell

Distribution messages: rationale for selecting one graph versus another

Distribution graph	Rationale for selecting particular graph
PIE 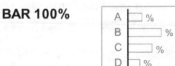	• Pie graphs are helpful to show relative differences among 3–6 groups of data—important to order the slices by size, starting with the biggest • The audience, however, can have difficulty quickly digesting pie graphs • Use a pie graph when your message centers on one particular group and fill only that slice with color to focus audience's attention
SINGLE STACKED COLUMN 100%	• Stacked column is a better illustration of relative differences between groups • Easier to layer on more data series by using text boxes to the right • Combine pie and single stacked graphs to tell two stories on one graph (see p. 89 for illustration)
COLUMN 100%	• Column distribution graphs are a very common way to show distribution (e.g., bell curve distribution is usually presented as a column graph) • Column format quickly makes biggest and smallest groups jump out for audience • Useful for wide range of number of groups (3–10 groups)
BAR 100%	• Bar version is more helpful if you want to layer on more data series by using text boxes to the right (see p. 87 for illustration) • Try to limit number of groups to include (fewer than 8 groups)
REFLECTION BAR 100%	• Reflection bar is simply two bar graphs combined into one and is useful if your message suggests a comparison of distributions for a common set of groups

Tracking time messages: rationale for selecting one graph versus another

Tracking time graph	Rationale for selecting particular graph
LINE	• Line graphs are useful if your message is about a change in something over a large number of time intervals • Better for messages for which audience does not need to know exact values at each time interval
COLUMN TIME	• Column time graphs are better when there is a smaller number of time intervals in your story (6 intervals or fewer) • If value at each interval is more important to your message, column time graphs make it easier to show value
MULTIPLE LINES	• Multiple line graphs are useful if your message is about change in multiple groups over a large number of time intervals • Effectively illustrates gaps between groups and points of interest, such as when lines cross each other (use callout boxes on p. 62 to label these interesting points)
DOUBLE COLUMN TIME	• Double time graph should be used only when you have a few time intervals • Helpful to show actual values of two groups changing over time
COLUMN TIME AND LINE	• Overlapping a line graph on a column graph is useful when you have two separate but related data series that you want to show on the same graph • Use two *y*-axes to describe two graphs • Do not use with a large number of time intervals

PowerPoint Presentations That Sell

Next, consider creating more advanced data graphs to combine two stories

Message type	Using text boxes to add second story	

Comparison

I want to compare two or more things

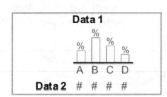

Start message with story from Data 1 and then expand to Data 2 insights on same groups (Company A has largest sales, but Company C has highest growth rate)

Distribution

I want to show how something breaks down into smaller pieces

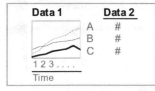

Story from Data 1 in column distribution can be enhanced by adding Data 2 series underneath (Business Unit B spends the highest proportion of R&D but has the lowest sales)

Track over time

I want to show a change in something over time

Highlight detail beyond change over time (Company A has the highest sales growth rate of X%)

How to create text boxes

- Click on "Text Box" icon in the Draw menu bar*

- Click on screen and type In numbers
- Align text boxes with data charts by selecting and moving with mouse

---

*Find the "Draw" menu by going to "View" → "Toolbars" → "Drawing" (see Part III for more details).

ILLUSTRATION: Example comparison message using minicase data

Message/research question

Thought process for choosing how to present data

Comparison

1. Which product had the most sales this year (TY)?
2. What was growth versus last year (LY)?

- Used bar graph to show relative difference between product sales
- Ordered graph from largest to smallest to quickly show the product with the most sales
- Used text boxes to right of bars to add second story about growth
- Put dotted rectangle around two data points to draw audience's attention since key learnings section references data points (see pp. 114 and 162)
- Used learning arrow to separate data and learnings (see p. 62)

Minicase data

	A	B	C	D	E
1		Sales ($ million)			% growth
2	Product	Last year (LY)	This year (TY)		TY vs LY
3	A	485	612		26.2%
4	B	716	765		6.9%
5	C	900	910		1.1%
6	D	123	149		20.9%
7	E	348	363		4.2%
8	Total	2,572	2,799		8.8%
9					
10		% of total sales			Change
11	Product	Last year (LY)	This year (TY)		TY vs LY
12	A	19%	22%		3%
13	B	27%	27%		0%
14	C	35%	33%		-2%
15	D	5%	5%		0%
16	E	14%	13%		-1%
17	Total	100%	100%		
18					
19	Product C by geography				
20	Region	This year (TY)	% of total		
21	East	91	10%		
22	West	373	41%		
23	North	182	20%		
24	South	264	29%		
25	Total	910	100%		

Example slide

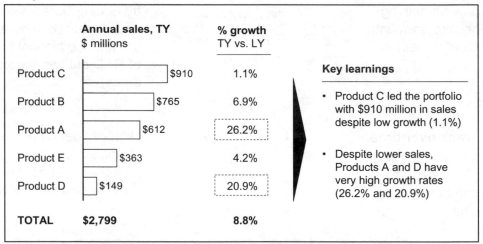

PowerPoint Presentations That Sell

ILLUSTRATION: Example distribution message using minicase data

Minicase data

	A	B	C	D	E
1		Sales ($ million)			% growth
2	Product	Last year (LY)	This year (TY)		TY vs LY
3	A	485	612		26.2%
4	B	716	765		6.9%
5	C	900	910		1.1%
6	D	123	149		20.9%
7	E	348	363		4.2%
8	Total	2,572	2,799		8.8%
9					
10		% of total sales			Change
11	Product	Last year (LY)	This year (TY)		TY vs LY
12	A	19%	22%		3%
13	B	27%	27%		0%
14	C	35%	33%		-2%
15	D	5%	5%		0%
16	E	14%	13%		-1%
17	Total	100%	100%		
18					
19	Product C by geography				
20	Region	This year (TY)	% of total		
21	East	91	10%		
22	West	373	41%		
23	North	182	20%		
24	South	264	29%		
25	Total	910	100%		

Message/research question

Distribution
1. How did this year's (TY) sales break down across products?
2. Break down across regions?

Thought process for choosing how to present data

- Used pie graph, ordered from largest slice to smallest, to show relative difference between products this year
- Decided to focus region analysis on biggest product—changed color of that product's slice to draw audience's attention (see pp. 116 and 171)
- Used single stacked 100% column to break down sales by region
- Used starburst on right to call out an insight (see p. 62 to create starburst)

Example slide

Breakdown of sales, TY
% of total sales

100% = $2,799 million

Prod D
Prod E 5%
13%
33% Prod C
Prod A
22%
27%
Prod B

Product C sales by region
% of sales

East	10%
North	20%
South	29%
West	41%
Product C	

Product C has highest proportion of sales, with majority in the West

ILLUSTRATION: Example time-tracking message using minicase data

Message/research question

Tracking over time

Did the distribution of sales across products change over time?

Thought process for choosing how to present data

- Used two stacked 100% column graphs to show breakdown of sales for each product for two different years
- Changed shading in graph of product that is called out in key learnings to draw audience's attention (see pp. 116 and 171)
- Used learning arrow to separate data and learnings (see p. 62)
- Used text boxes to right of columns to add second story about change in sales share

Minicase data

	A	B	C	D	E
1		Sales ($ million)			% growth
2	Product	Last year (LY)	This year (TY)		TY vs LY
3	A	485	612		26.2%
4	B	716	765		6.9%
5	C	900	910		1.1%
6	D	123	149		20.9%
7	E	348	363		4.2%
8	Total	2,572	2,799		8.8%
9					
10		% of total sales			Change
11	Product	Last year (LY)	This year (TY)		TY vs LY
12	A	19%	22%		3%
13	B	27%	27%		0%
14	C	35%	33%		-2%
15	D	5%	5%		0%
16	E	14%	13%		-1%
17	Total	100%	100%		
18					
19	Product C by geography				
20	Region	This year (TY)	% of total		
21	East	91	10%		
22	West	373	41%		
23	North	182	20%		
24	South	264	29%		
25	Total	910	100%		

Example slide

Breakdown of sales
% of total sales

Change in share

Key learnings

100% = $2,572 $2,799

	Last year	This year	Change in share
Product D	5%	5%	–
Product E	14%	13%	–1%
Product A	19%	22%	+3%
Product B	27%	27%	–
Product C	35%	33%	–2%

Last year — This year

- Although Product A has taken share, Product B still accounts for higher proportion of total sales
- Product C (the firm's most profitable product) has lost share—potentially need to increase budget allocation

PowerPoint Presentations That Sell

Summary of what to think about when creating a data-driven slide

4	**Four steps for consistent, action-oriented slides (from p. 43)** • *Slide message:* What message or mini-story am I trying to convey on this slide? • *Action-oriented:* Does my slide message lead to action? If not, what additional information is needed? • *Effective communication:* Does my slide structure effectively communicate my message? If not, what other geometric shapes could improve the communication? • *Necessary information:* Are all the data points on the slide necessary to defend my recommendations? If not, delete unnecessary information
5	**Five audience data slide–related questions to answer (from p. 77)** • What are the insights from the data that I care about? • Which key data point(s) should I be looking at on the slide? • What data am I looking at (e.g., data graph title/description and units)? • In a large set of data, which data series is the biggest and which is smallest? • How much have the numbers in the chart changed over time (i.e., percentage change year over year) or compared to something else?
3	**Three slide elements to introduce, reveal, and support story (from p. 78)** • *Slide title:* Introduces mini-story and gets audience excited about reading the rest of the slide by providing some specific insight into the situation • *Learnings/recommendations:* Reveals your interesting learnings directly on the slide rather than just as talking points; do not just repeat data already on the slide • *Supporting data analysis:* Drives the insights that lead to actionable recommendations while providing assurance to the audience that there is factual support for the recommendations

Chapter 7 Creating Compelling Graphs with Data

Simple techniques to plan, design, and deliver presentations that get results

Chapter 7 provides specific step-by-step instructions for creating data charts and understanding which chart is optimal, based on the type of data you are presenting. It addresses common scenarios, or message types conveyed in presentations, such as using data to make a comparison, illustrate distribution or process flow, or show how something changes over time. Screenshots are used to illustrate ways to create and format graphs in Excel and then paste them into PowerPoint.

What's next: Actually creating data graphs

What's next

Create data graphs from scratch

- Step-by-step instructions for creating data graphs (including illustrations of how to create graphs in Excel)
- Instructions for pasting graph from Excel into PowerPoint

What you've done

You have learned how to choose which type of data graph to use, based on the message you want to deliver

Use "emphasizing" and "formatting" principles

- Illustrations with step-by-step instructions to emphasize data graphs to maximize impact
- Illustrations with step-by-step instructions to format data graphs to draw audience's attention to the most important information

Creating data graphs from scratch by using Excel

**Approach to creating graphs from scratch
covered in the following pages**

 Set up your data in Excel as a data table
Put data in column format and order data
for graph

 **Create graph by using Excel's "Chart
Wizard"**
Four-step process to create desired graph

③ **Reformat graph to make it presentation-
ready**
Remove unnecessary color and lines from
graph

④ **Copy and paste graph from Excel into
PowerPoint**
Instructions to copy and paste and resize
graph

Next set of pages details
the step-by-step instructions
for creating presentation-
ready graphs

Pages are written so that
you can practice each step
of the process—open Excel
and PowerPoint to practice

Step 1: Set up your data in Excel as a data table

First column in Excel data table should be the list of items you want in the graph (products, regions, time periods, financial labels, etc.)

Second column in Excel data table should be actual data that correspond to each item in your list

	A	B	C	D
1				
2		Item		
3		A		
4		B		
5		C		
6		D		
7		E		
8				

	A	B	C	D
1				
2		Item	Sales	
3		A	100	
4		B	150	
5		C	75	
6		D	250	
7		E	50	
8				

Note:
- Putting data in this column format (i.e., one type of data in column B and another type in column C) makes it easier to create graph (rather than putting each type of data in rows)
- Make sure your data table does not have any blank rows or blank columns (i.e., in the two data type examples above, if "Item" data is in column B, "Data" should be in column C, not column D)

PowerPoint Presentations That Sell

Step 1 continued: Reorder your data if desired

To reorder:
- Highlight cells (including top row of labels)
- Select the "Data" menu
- Click "Sort"

- Sort by your "Sales" column
- In either ascending or descending order (see note below for guidance)
- Select "Header row"
- Click OK

Resulting reordered data table

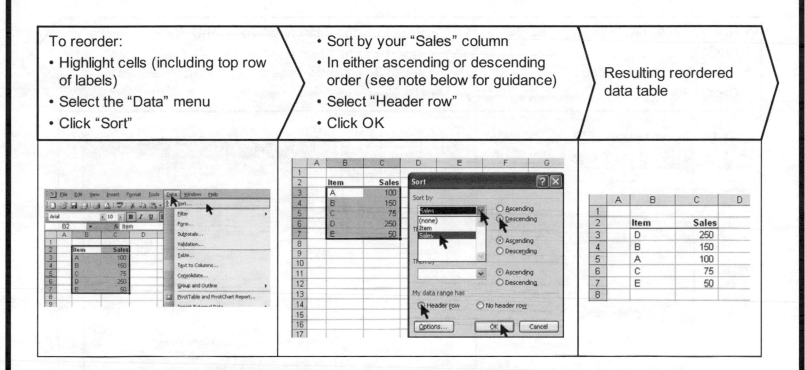

Note:
- Order of items in data table will be order of items in your data graph, so decide what order you want ahead of time
- Putting data in order from biggest to smallest is usually best when you are comparing items with each other because audience can quickly see relative differences (see p. 117 for more details)

Step 2a: Create graph by using Excel's "Chart Wizard"

- Highlight cells (including top row of labels)
- Select the "Insert" menu
- Click "Chart"

- Select which "Chart type" you want
- Select which "Chart sub-type" you want (do not select 3-D graphs—see p. 127 for more details)
- Hit "Next"

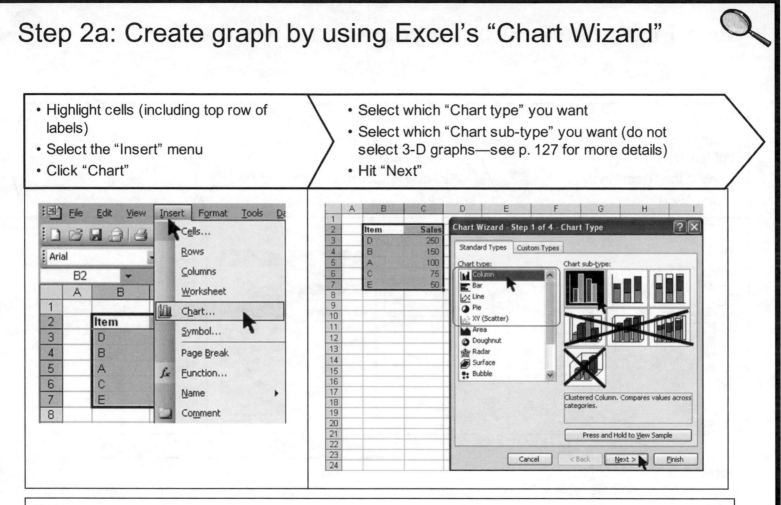

Note:
- Use "Chart sub-type" on the right side of the Chart Wizard's Step 1 of 4 to select additional types of graphs, such as "Stacked Bar" and "Single Stacked Column 100%"
- See Chapter 6 to decide which chart to use

Note: See Appendix A for corresponding screenshots for PowerPoint 2007.

PowerPoint Presentations That Sell

Step 2b: Select "Series" tab and pull in graph's source data

- In Chart Wizard's Step 2 of 4, select "Series" tab
- Use "Values" for your data columns (e.g., "Sales" from example) and "Category axis labels" for nondata description column (e.g., "Item" from example)
- Use "Name" field to title each data series
- Hit "Next"

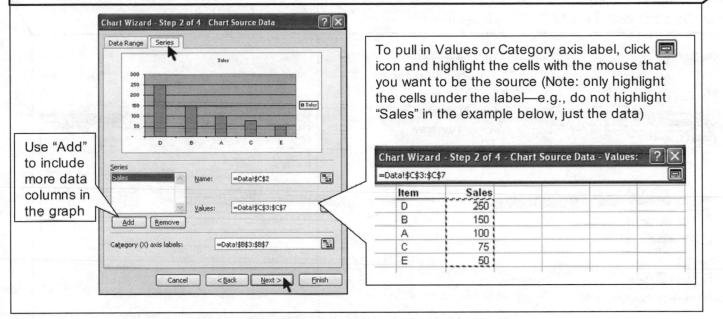

To pull in Values or Category axis label, click icon and highlight the cells with the mouse that you want to be the source (Note: only highlight the cells under the label—e.g., do not highlight "Sales" in the example below, just the data)

Use "Add" to include more data columns in the graph

Note:
- To return to this dialog box once you initially create a graph, right click on the created graph and select "Source Data..."

Note: See Appendix A for corresponding screenshots for PowerPoint 2007.

Step 2c and 2d: Format graph and place in spreadsheet

Format graph in Chart Wizard's Step 3 of 4 by using each tab:
- In "Title" tab, leave all title fields blank (will add in PowerPoint by using text boxes)
- In "Axis" tab, uncheck *y*-axis (will replace with values)
- In "Gridlines" tab, uncheck all gridlines (reduces clutter on graph)
- In "Legends" tab, uncheck legend (can add back in PowerPoint)
- In "Data Labels," check "Value" (replaces need for *y*-axis)

In Chart Wizard's Step 4 of 4:
- Select "As object in:" option to place graph in the spreadsheet so that you can copy it into PowerPoint
- Hit "Finish"

Chart title:

Category (X) axis:

Value (Y) axis:

Primary axis
- ☑ Category (X) axis
  - ⦿ Automatic
  - ○ Category
  - ○ Time-scale
- ☐ Value (Y) axis

Category (X) axis
- ☐ Major gridlines
- ☐ Minor gridlines

Value (Y) axis
- ☐ Major gridlines
- ☐ Minor gridlines

☐ Show legend

Label Contains
- ☐ Series name
- ☐ Category name
- ☑ Value

Chart Wizard - Step 4 of 4 - Chart Location   [?][X]

Place chart:

○ As new sheet: Chart1

○ As object in: Data

Cancel   < Back   Next >   Finish

Note:
- The guidance above can be used for each type of graph (column, bar, pie, line), although the options for each type will differ slightly

Note: See Appendix A for corresponding screenshots for PowerPoint 2007.

Step 3: Reformat graph to make it presentation-ready

- Use steps A–G below to reformat graph by removing unnecessary color and lines
- Guidance on previous page (Step 2c) covers some of these steps

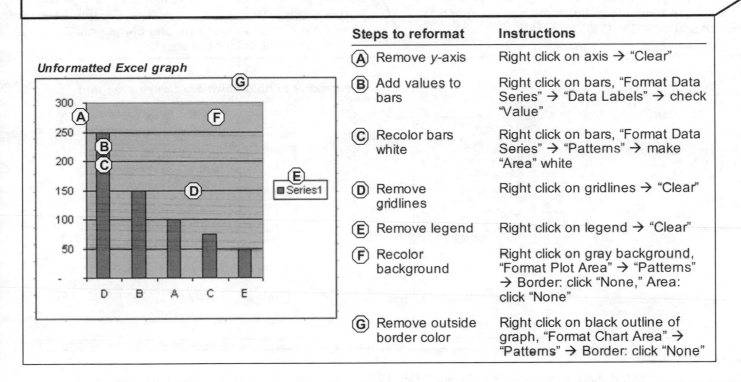

Unformatted Excel graph

Steps to reformat	Instructions
(A) Remove *y*-axis	Right click on axis → "Clear"
(B) Add values to bars	Right click on bars, "Format Data Series" → "Data Labels" → check "Value"
(C) Recolor bars white	Right click on bars, "Format Data Series" → "Patterns" → make "Area" white
(D) Remove gridlines	Right click on gridlines → "Clear"
(E) Remove legend	Right click on legend → "Clear"
(F) Recolor background	Right click on gray background, "Format Plot Area" → "Patterns" → Border: click "None," Area: click "None"
(G) Remove outside border color	Right click on black outline of graph, "Format Chart Area" → "Patterns" → Border: click "None"

Note:
- The guidance above can be used for each type of graph (column, bar, pie, line)

Step 4: Copy and paste graph from Excel into PowerPoint

- Right click mouse on one of the graph's corners and click "Copy"
- Alternatively, you can select the graph by clicking the mouse near one of the corners of the graph in Excel and click Ctrl+C to copy

- Paste graph into PowerPoint by clicking Ctrl+V
- Alternatively, you can paste the graph as an image to not allow editing by going to "Edit" → "Paste Special…" → "Picture (Windows Metafile)" and hit OK
- Resize graph in PowerPoint by selecting graph, hold down Shift key, click mouse on one of the graph's corners, and drag to desired size

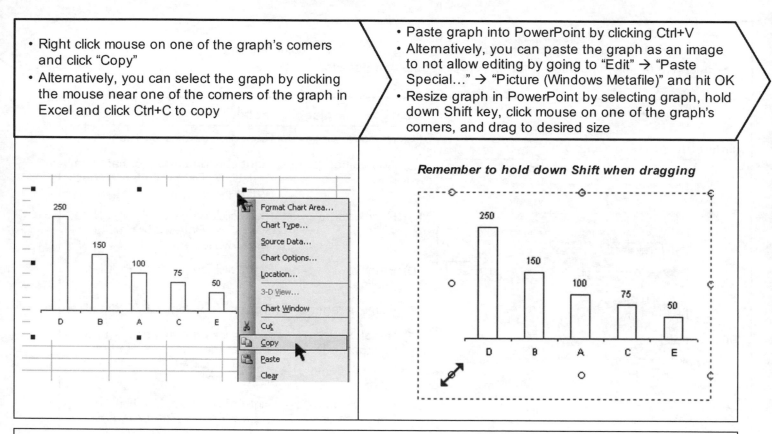

Remember to hold down Shift when dragging

Note:
- Once you've pasted the Excel graph into PowerPoint, include text callouts such as "key learnings" on the slide
- See Chapter 8 for additional "emphasizing" and "formatting" principles to maximize the impact of the data graph

Chapter 8 Improving Presentation of Data

Simple techniques to plan, design, and deliver presentations that get results

Chapter 8 offers over 20 "emphasizing" and "formatting" principles to improve the presentation of your data. Emphasizing principles, which are categorized as "learning callouts," "attention grabbers," "guess prevention," and "data accents," are meant to draw audience's attention to most important information on a slide. Formatting principles, categorized as "clutter reduction," "descriptive," and "eye pleasing," help you simplify the presentation of your data to focus attention on the slide's key information. At the end of this chapter, there is one page for each principle detailing specific recommendations with before-and-after illustrations.

Use "emphasizing" and "formatting" principles to maximize the impact of data graphs

"Emphasizing" principles*

- Emphasizing principles are meant to draw the audience's attention to the most important information

- Type of principles include:
  - "Learning callout"
  - "Attention grabbers"
  - "Guess prevention"
  - "Data accents"

- Answers many of the audience members' questions before they have a chance to ask, including
  - What are the insights?
  - Which data should I look at?
  - Which is biggest/smallest?
  - How much has data changed?

- **Next three pages outline these principles**

- **Following pages illustrate each principle with step-by-step instructions**

"Formatting" principles*

- Formatting principles simplify the presentation of data to focus attention on key information

- Creates more white space on chart

- Type of principles include:
  - "Clutter reduction"
  - "Descriptive"
  - "Eye pleasing"

- Answers other audience question about "which data am I looking at?"

*The details of these principles are outlined on the next few pages and then illustrated on the pages that follow.

PowerPoint Presentations That Sell

Emphasizing and formatting principles* improve both the quality of the message and the appearance of the slide

□ Principle

Emphasizing and formatting principles* across improvements of message quality and appearance

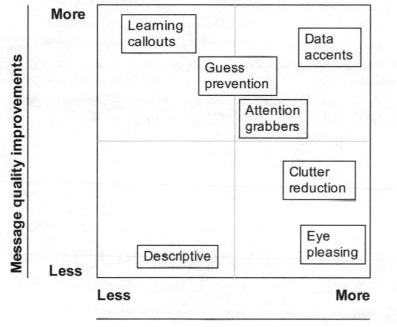

Considerations

- Important to consider using each of these principles when making slides

- After completing a set of slides, ask yourself, "Can I use any of these principles to improve either my message or my slide's look?"

*Emphasizing and formatting principles are detailed on the next few pages.

Use "emphasizing principles" to maximize impact

	Guidance	Benefit	Illus-tration
Learning callout	• Includes key learnings as text on data graph slides to draw attention to insights (but don't just summarize graph's data)	→ Answers key audience question— "What are the insights from this data?"	p. 113
Attention grabbers	• Call attention to key information on graph with shaded/dashed boxes	→ Answers key audience question— "Which data point(s) should I look at?"	p. 114
	• Maintain white space around data table to include comments in callout boxes to call attention to data's relevance	→ Answers key audience question— "What are the insights from this data?"	p. 115
	• Use color/shading to highlight only key data series, not to differentiate all data series—put other bars or pie slices in white	→ Simplifies what audience needs to focus on	p. 116
Guess prevention	• Order data from biggest to smallest in bar/column graphs	→ Answers key audience question— "Which data is the biggest/smallest?"	p. 117
	• Calculate change between numbers (e.g., 20% increase) rather than just showing absolute data points (e.g., $50 and $60)	→ Change in numbers is often more insightful	p. 118
Data accents	• Illustrate percent changes with lines and arrows	→ Quickly reveals change in data	p. 119
	• Use dashed lines to label average of data points and bold text boxes for total summation	→ Averages and totals are helpful benchmarks to make comparisons	p. 120

PowerPoint Presentations That Sell

Use "formatting principles" to simplify the presentation of data and focus attention on key content

	Guidance	Benefit	Illus-tration
Clutter reduction	• Reduce amount of information on nondata part of graph (graph background color and lines)	→ Reduces unnecessary visual clutter on graph	p. 121
	• Adjust the gap between columns/bars in graphs to create more white space	→ More white space between columns/bars can make graph more readable	p. 122
	• If showing 2–3 data series on bar/column graph, use legend in top right of slide to label series	→ More space-efficient than labeling the series on each bar/column	p. 123
	• On line graphs, avoid using legends—instead, put name of data right next to end of line	→ Easier for audience to see which data series aligns with each line on graph	p. 124
	• On graphs, minimize use of decimals on the *x*-axis and *y*-axis but use commas for large numbers	→ Decimals on axes take up extra space while not adding value	p. 125
	• On tables, minimize number of decimals (especially after first decimal) unless it is necessary because of data's scale	→ Extra decimals (1,000.2, 5.436) unnecessarily suggest data is precise while cluttering table	p. 126
	• Use basic style instead of 3-D graph style	→ Reduces complexity of graph look	p. 127

Use "formatting principles" to simplify presentation of data and focus attention on key content (CONTINUED)

	Guidance	Benefit	Illus-tration
Descriptive	• Include graph title and units, aligned directly above graph on left side, in addition to including units on graph data, if possible	→ Answers the audience's first question about graph—"What am I looking at?"	p. 128
Eye pleasing	• On tables, bold and right align all column headings since data is automatically right aligned in Excel	→ Answers the audience's first question about the table—"What am I looking at?" and it is easier for audience to read when heading is aligned with data	p. 129

Emphasizing Principle—Learning Callout:
Include learnings directly on slide

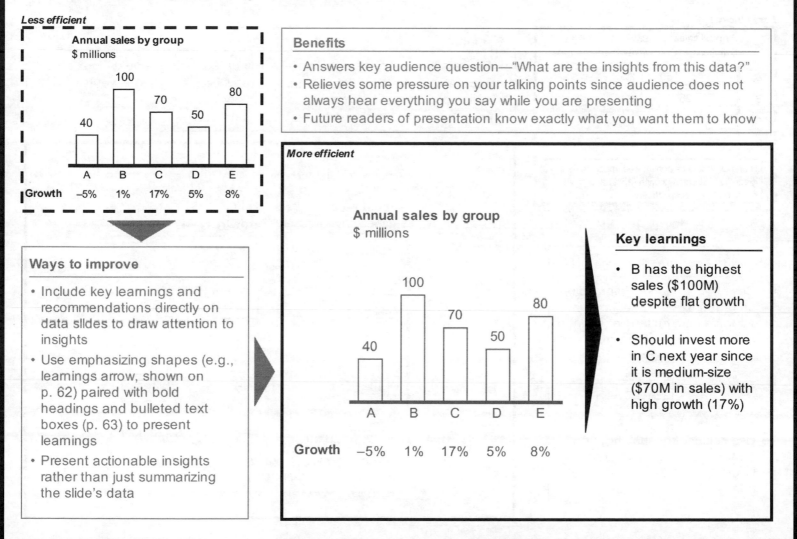

Less efficient

Annual sales by group
$ millions

	A	B	C	D	E
Sales	40	100	70	50	80
Growth	–5%	1%	17%	5%	8%

Benefits

- Answers key audience question—"What are the insights from this data?"
- Relieves some pressure on your talking points since audience does not always hear everything you say while you are presenting
- Future readers of presentation know exactly what you want them to know

Ways to improve

- Include key learnings and recommendations directly on data slides to draw attention to insights
- Use emphasizing shapes (e.g., learnings arrow, shown on p. 62) paired with bold headings and bulleted text boxes (p. 63) to present learnings
- Present actionable insights rather than just summarizing the slide's data

More efficient

Annual sales by group
$ millions

	A	B	C	D	E
Sales	40	100	70	50	80
Growth	–5%	1%	17%	5%	8%

Key learnings

- B has the highest sales ($100M) despite flat growth

- Should invest more in C next year since it is medium-size ($70M in sales) with high growth (17%)

Emphasizing Principle—Attention Grabbers:
Use shaded/dashed boxes to call attention to important information

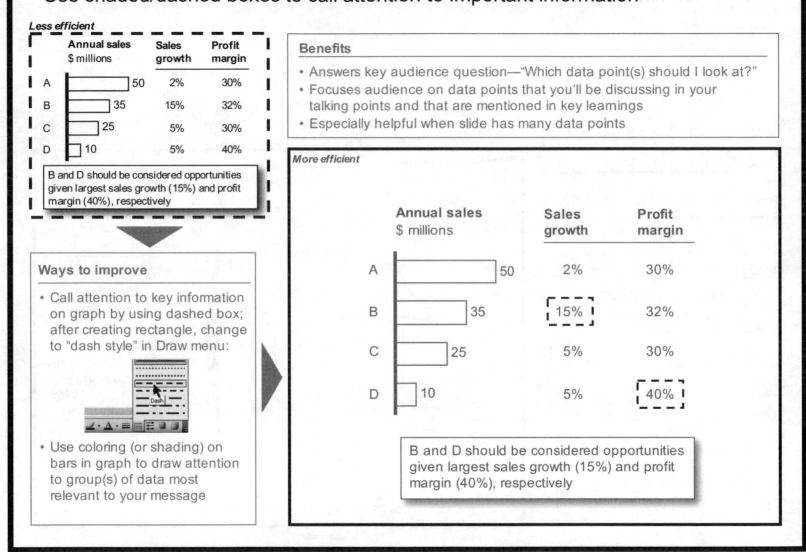

Less efficient

Annual sales $ millions	Sales growth	Profit margin
A 50	2%	30%
B 35	15%	32%
C 25	5%	30%
D 10	5%	40%

B and D should be considered opportunities given largest sales growth (15%) and profit margin (40%), respectively

Benefits

- Answers key audience question—"Which data point(s) should I look at?"
- Focuses audience on data points that you'll be discussing in your talking points and that are mentioned in key learnings
- Especially helpful when slide has many data points

More efficient

Annual sales $ millions	Sales growth	Profit margin
A 50	2%	30%
B 35	15%	32%
C 25	5%	30%
D 10	5%	40%

B and D should be considered opportunities given largest sales growth (15%) and profit margin (40%), respectively

Ways to improve

- Call attention to key information on graph by using dashed box; after creating rectangle, change to "dash style" in Draw menu:

- Use coloring (or shading) on bars in graph to draw attention to group(s) of data most relevant to your message

Emphasizing Principle—Attention Grabbers:
Use callout boxes to highlight key data points in table

Less efficient

Continent	Population (in millions)			30-yr growth rate	
	1970	2000	2030	1970–2000	2000–2030
Asia	2,158	3,676	4,978	70%	35%
Africa	361	800	1,461	121%	83%
Europe	658	731	702	11%	−4%
North America	321	485	644	51%	33%
South America	191	348	463	82%	33%
Oceania	19	31	41	59%	34%
WORLD	3,708	6,072	8,290	64%	37%

Source U.S. Census Bureau, International Database.

Benefits

- Answers key audience questions—"What are the insights from this data?" and "Which data point(s) should I look at on the slide?"
- Focuses audience on data points you'll be discussing in your talking points (i.e., audience could cover up data table and still see what's important)

Ways to improve

- Maintain white space around data table (and graphs) to include comments
- Callout box is a useful tool to include these comments and calls attention to data's relevance
- See p. 62 for details on how to create callout boxes and p. 145 for how to format text within boxes

More efficient

Asia has the highest population

EU is only continent with negative growth

Continent	Population (in millions)			30-yr growth rate	
	1970	2000	2030	1970–2000	2000–2030
Asia	2,158	3,676	4,978	70%	35%
Africa	361	800	1,461	121%	83%
Europe	658	731	702	11%	−4%
North America	321	485	644	51%	33%
South America	191	348	463	82%	33%
Oceania	19	31	41	59%	34%
WORLD	3,708	6,072	8,290	64%	37

Population growth is slowing across all continents

Source U.S. Census Bureau, International Database.

Emphasizing Principle—Attention Grabbers:
Use color and shading to highlight only key data, not every data point

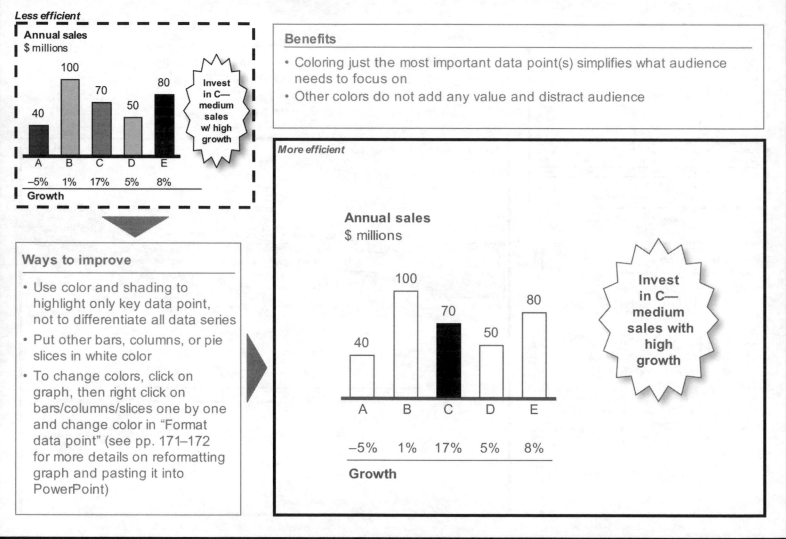

Less efficient

Annual sales
$ millions

100

80

70

50

40

A B C D E

–5% 1% 17% 5% 8%

Growth

Invest in C—medium sales w/ high growth

Benefits

- Coloring just the most important data point(s) simplifies what audience needs to focus on
- Other colors do not add any value and distract audience

Ways to improve

- Use color and shading to highlight only key data point, not to differentiate all data series
- Put other bars, columns, or pie slices in white color
- To change colors, click on graph, then right click on bars/columns/slices one by one and change color in "Format data point" (see pp. 171–172 for more details on reformatting graph and pasting it into PowerPoint)

More efficient

Annual sales
$ millions

100

80

70

50

40

A B C D E

–5% 1% 17% 5% 8%

Growth

Invest in C—medium sales with high growth

Emphasizing Principle—Guess Prevention:
Order data points from biggest to smallest

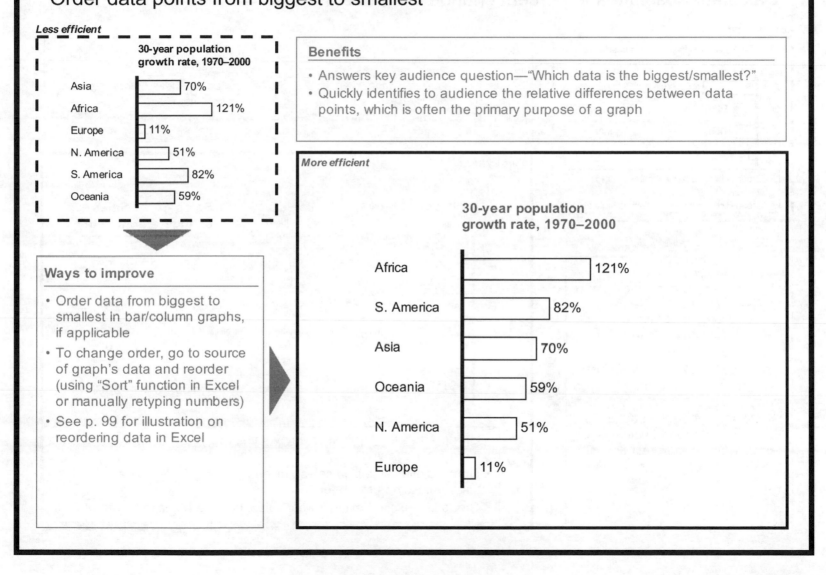

Less efficient

30-year population growth rate, 1970–2000

Asia	70%
Africa	121%
Europe	11%
N. America	51%
S. America	82%
Oceania	59%

Ways to improve

- Order data from biggest to smallest in bar/column graphs, if applicable
- To change order, go to source of graph's data and reorder (using "Sort" function in Excel or manually retyping numbers)
- See p. 99 for illustration on reordering data in Excel

Benefits

- Answers key audience question—"Which data is the biggest/smallest?"
- Quickly identifies to audience the relative differences between data points, which is often the primary purpose of a graph

More efficient

30-year population growth rate, 1970–2000

Africa	121%
S. America	82%
Asia	70%
Oceania	59%
N. America	51%
Europe	11%

Emphasizing Principle—Guess Prevention:
Calculate absolute and percent change in numbers

Less efficient

	This year's sales $ millions	Last year's sales $ millions
A	$1,050	$1,000
B	$450	$350
C	$400	$400
D	$150	$100

- Group A has the biggest sales over last two years
- Group B overcame C as second highest

Ways to improve

- Calculate change between numbers rather than just showing absolute data
- Calculate percent change (e.g., 20% increase) rather than just the absolute numbers (e.g., $60 and $50)
- To include change in numbers on slide, either add columns to data tables or add text boxes to the right of data graphs (see p. 151 for instructions)

Benefits

- Answers key audience question—"How much have numbers changed?"
- Change in numbers is especially helpful if your message focuses on change
- Percent change in numbers is more insightful because it normalizes the differences between data with wide range of magnitudes (e.g., a change of $50 is a 5% increase for sales of $1,000 but a 50% increase for sales of $100)

More efficient

	This year's sales $ millions	Last year's sales $ millions	Sales change	Sales growth
A	$1,050	$1,000	$50	5%
B	$450	$350	$100	29%
C	$400	$400	$0	0%
D	$150	$100	$50	50%

- Group A has the biggest sales over last two years but has experienced slow growth
- Group B overcame C in sales, driven by almost 30% increase in sales versus no growth for C
- Group D, despite having lowest sales, has the highest growth at 50%

PowerPoint Presentations That Sell

Emphasizing Principle—Data Accents:
Illustrate percent change with lines and arrows

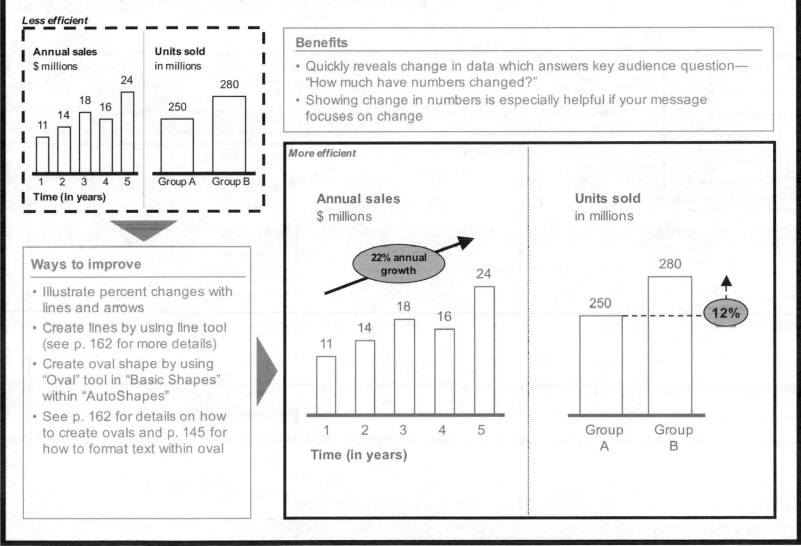

Less efficient

Annual sales
$ millions

24
18
16
14
11

1 2 3 4 5
Time (in years)

Units sold
in millions

280
250

Group A   Group B

Benefits

- Quickly reveals change in data which answers key audience question— "How much have numbers changed?"
- Showing change in numbers is especially helpful if your message focuses on change

Ways to improve

- Illustrate percent changes with lines and arrows
- Create lines by using line tool (see p. 162 for more details)
- Create oval shape by using "Oval" tool in "Basic Shapes" within "AutoShapes"
- See p. 162 for details on how to create ovals and p. 145 for how to format text within oval

More efficient

Annual sales
$ millions

22% annual growth

24
18
16
14
11

1 2 3 4 5
Time (in years)

Units sold
in millions

280
250
12%

Group A   Group B

Emphasizing Principle—Data Accents:
Use dotted lines and bold text for averages and totals

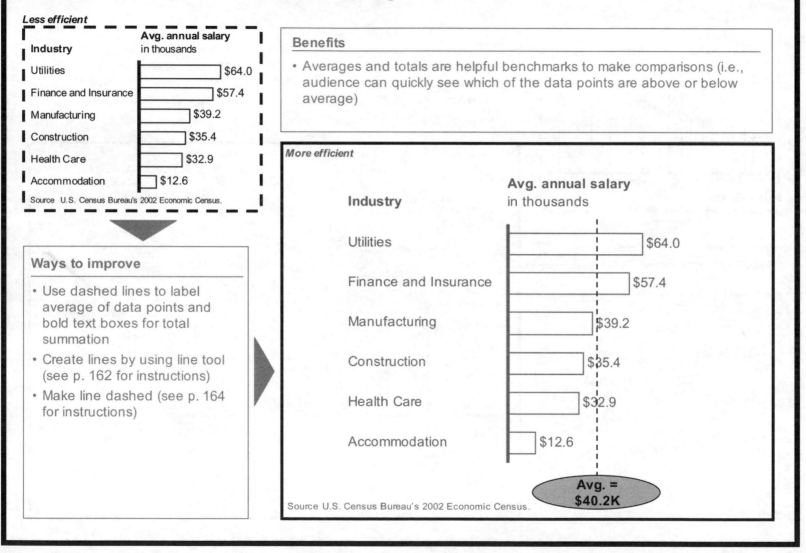

Less efficient

Industry	Avg. annual salary in thousands
Utilities	$64.0
Finance and Insurance	$57.4
Manufacturing	$39.2
Construction	$35.4
Health Care	$32.9
Accommodation	$12.6

Source U.S. Census Bureau's 2002 Economic Census.

Benefits

• Averages and totals are helpful benchmarks to make comparisons (i.e., audience can quickly see which of the data points are above or below average)

Ways to improve

• Use dashed lines to label average of data points and bold text boxes for total summation

• Create lines by using line tool (see p. 162 for instructions)

• Make line dashed (see p. 164 for instructions)

More efficient

Industry	Avg. annual salary in thousands
Utilities	$64.0
Finance and Insurance	$57.4
Manufacturing	$39.2
Construction	$35.4
Health Care	$32.9
Accommodation	$12.6

Avg. = $40.2K

Source U.S. Census Bureau's 2002 Economic Census.

Formatting Principle—Clutter Reduction:
Eliminate background color and lines

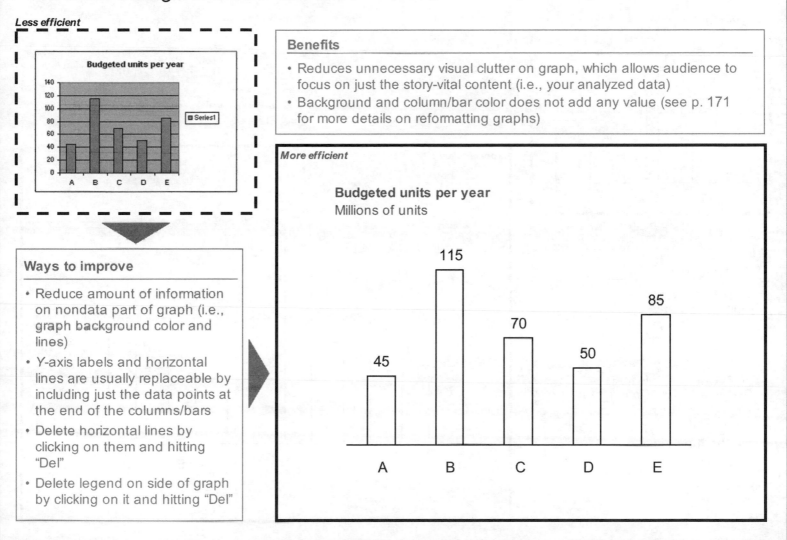

Less efficient

Budgeted units per year

Ways to improve

- Reduce amount of information on nondata part of graph (i.e., graph background color and lines)
- Y-axis labels and horizontal lines are usually replaceable by including just the data points at the end of the columns/bars
- Delete horizontal lines by clicking on them and hitting "Del"
- Delete legend on side of graph by clicking on it and hitting "Del"

Benefits

- Reduces unnecessary visual clutter on graph, which allows audience to focus on just the story-vital content (i.e., your analyzed data)
- Background and column/bar color does not add any value (see p. 171 for more details on reformatting graphs)

More efficient

Budgeted units per year
Millions of units

	115			85
45		70	50	
A	B	C	D	E

Formatting Principle—Clutter Reduction:
Adjust width of columns and bars to create more space

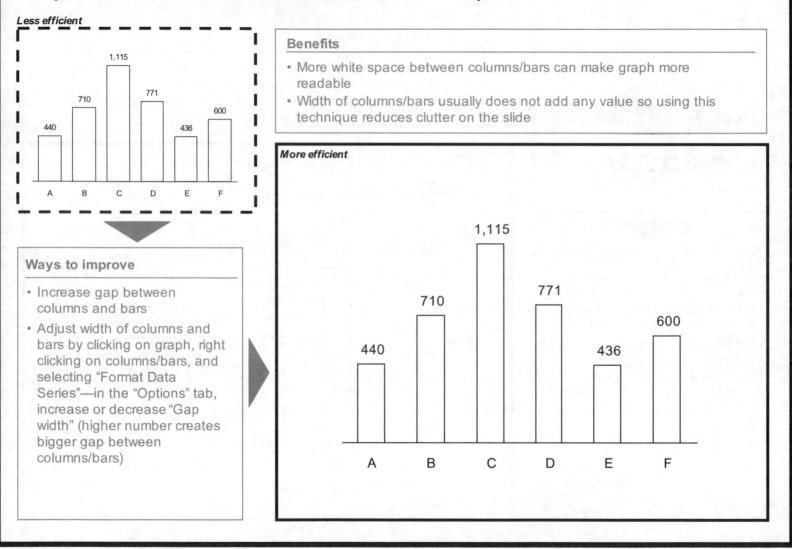

Less efficient

Benefits

- More white space between columns/bars can make graph more readable
- Width of columns/bars usually does not add any value so using this technique reduces clutter on the slide

Ways to improve

- Increase gap between columns and bars
- Adjust width of columns and bars by clicking on graph, right clicking on columns/bars, and selecting "Format Data Series"—in the "Options" tab, increase or decrease "Gap width" (higher number creates bigger gap between columns/bars)

More efficient

Formatting Principle—Clutter Reduction:
Put legend in top right corner

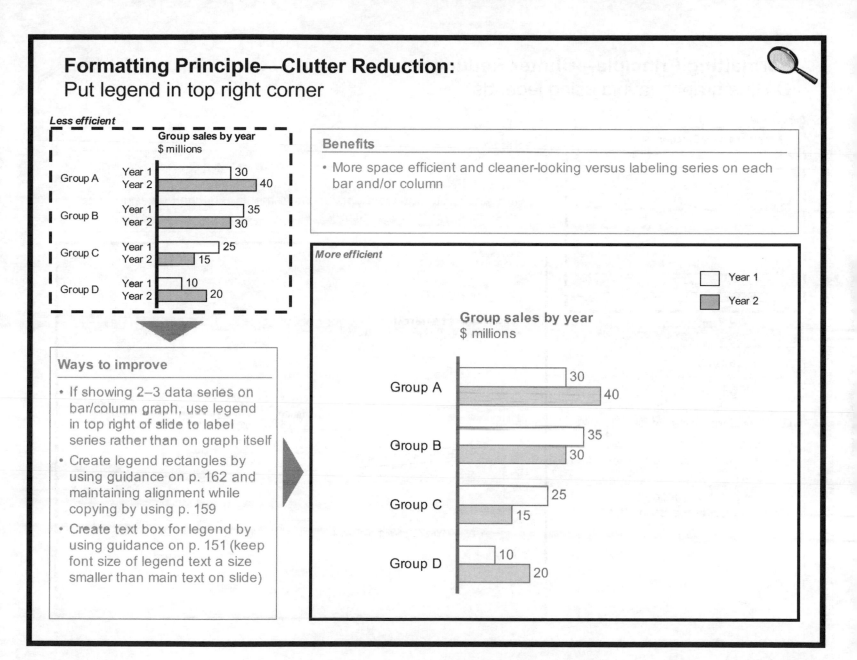

Less efficient

Group sales by year
$ millions

Group A	Year 1	30
	Year 2	40
Group B	Year 1	35
	Year 2	30
Group C	Year 1	25
	Year 2	15
Group D	Year 1	10
	Year 2	20

Benefits

• More space efficient and cleaner-looking versus labeling series on each bar and/or column

Ways to improve

• If showing 2–3 data series on bar/column graph, use legend in top right of slide to label series rather than on graph itself

• Create legend rectangles by using guidance on p. 162 and maintaining alignment while copying by using p. 159

• Create text box for legend by using guidance on p. 151 (keep font size of legend text a size smaller than main text on slide)

More efficient

Year 1
Year 2

Group sales by year
$ millions

- Group A: 30 / 40
- Group B: 35 / 30
- Group C: 25 / 15
- Group D: 10 / 20

Formatting Principle—Clutter Reduction:
On line graphs, avoid using legends

Less efficient

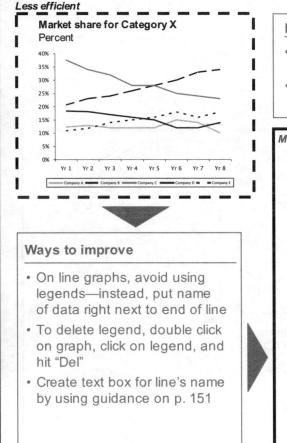

Market share for Category X
Percent

Benefits

- Much easier for audience to see which data series aligns with each line on graph
- Offers option to add more data series to the right of chart by using text boxes (see p. 87 for illustration)

More efficient

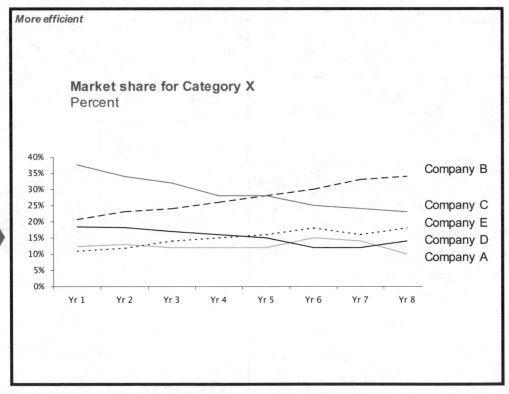

Market share for Category X
Percent

Ways to improve

- On line graphs, avoid using legends—instead, put name of data right next to end of line
- To delete legend, double click on graph, click on legend, and hit "Del"
- Create text box for line's name by using guidance on p. 151

Formatting Principle—Clutter Reduction:
Minimize decimal usage on graph axes but use commas

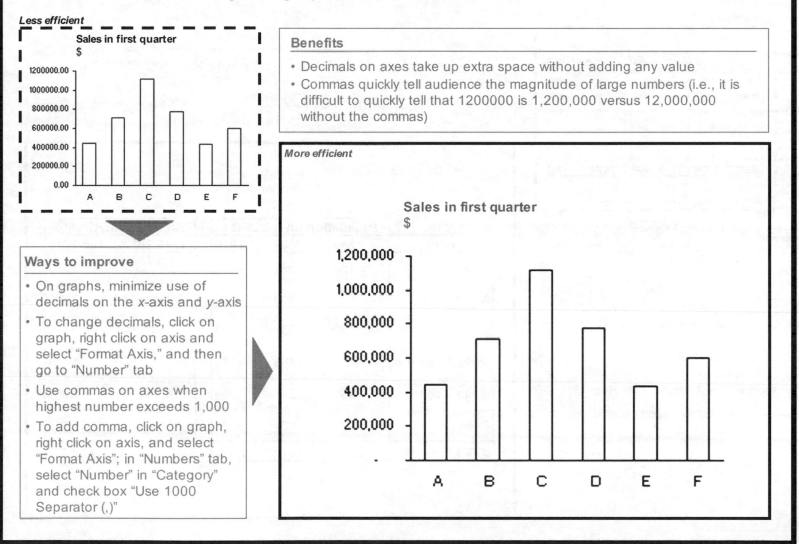

Less efficient

Sales in first quarter
$

Benefits

- Decimals on axes take up extra space without adding any value
- Commas quickly tell audience the magnitude of large numbers (i.e., it is difficult to quickly tell that 1200000 is 1,200,000 versus 12,000,000 without the commas)

More efficient

Sales in first quarter
$

Ways to improve

- On graphs, minimize use of decimals on the *x*-axis and *y*-axis
- To change decimals, click on graph, right click on axis and select "Format Axis," and then go to "Number" tab
- Use commas on axes when highest number exceeds 1,000
- To add comma, click on graph, right click on axis, and select "Format Axis"; in "Numbers" tab, select "Number" in "Category" and check box "Use 1000 Separator (,)"

Formatting Principle—Clutter Reduction:
On tables, minimize number of decimals

Less efficient

Continent	Population (in millions)			Annual growth rate	
	1990	2000	2010	1990–2000	2000–2010
Asia	3,180.3	3,676.1	4,143.2	1.46%	1.20%
Africa	624.2	800.1	996.5	2.51%	2.22%
Europe	722.5	731.4	728.8	0.12%	−0.04%
North America	423.4	485.1	539.1	1.37%	1.06%
South America	296.4	348.3	392.6	1.62%	1.21%
Oceania	26.6	30.8	34.7	1.47%	1.21%
WORLD	**5,273.4**	**6,071.7**	**6,834.9**	**1.42%**	**1.19%**

Source U.S. Census Bureau, International Database.

Benefits

- Extra decimals (e.g., 1,000.2, 5.436%) usually do not add anything to the message
- Also, decimals unnecessarily suggest data is precise while cluttering table
- This logic also applies to data shown in graphs

Ways to improve

- On tables, minimize number of decimals (especially after first decimal) unless it is necessary because of data's scale
- If in Excel, click on cell with too many decimals and click "Decrease Decimal" button,

or right click on cell and click "Format Cell"; go to "Number" tab and change "Decimal places"

More efficient

Continent	Population (in millions)			Annual growth rate	
	1990	2000	2010	1990-2000	2000-2010
Asia	3,180	3,676	4,143	1.5%	1.2%
Africa	624	800	997	2.5%	2.2%
Europe	723	731	729	0.1%	0.0%
North America	423	485	539	1.4%	1.1%
South America	296	348	393	1.6%	1.2%
Oceania	27	31	35	1.5%	1.2%
WORLD	**5,273**	**6,072**	**6,835**	**1.4%**	**1.2%**

Source U.S. Census Bureau, International Database.

PowerPoint Presentations That Sell

Formatting Principle—Clutter Reduction:
Use basic column graph instead of 3-D graph style

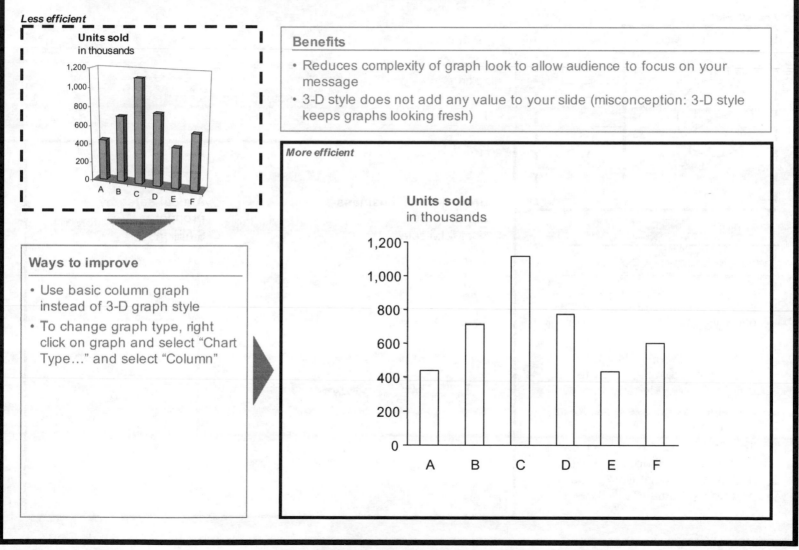

Less efficient

Units sold
in thousands

Benefits

- Reduces complexity of graph look to allow audience to focus on your message
- 3-D style does not add any value to your slide (misconception: 3-D style keeps graphs looking fresh)

More efficient

Ways to improve

- Use basic column graph instead of 3-D graph style
- To change graph type, right click on graph and select "Chart Type…" and select "Column"

Units sold
in thousands

Formatting Principle—Descriptive:
Include graph title with units and also units on graph

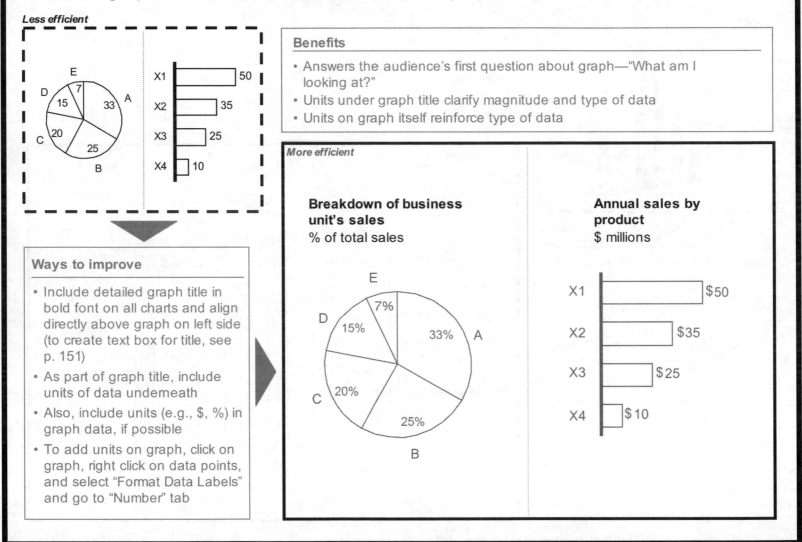

Less efficient

E
D 7
15 33 A
C 20
25
B

X1 ▭ 50
X2 ▭ 35
X3 ▭ 25
X4 ▯ 10

Benefits

- Answers the audience's first question about graph—"What am I looking at?"
- Units under graph title clarify magnitude and type of data
- Units on graph itself reinforce type of data

Ways to improve

- Include detailed graph title in bold font on all charts and align directly above graph on left side (to create text box for title, see p. 151)
- As part of graph title, include units of data underneath
- Also, include units (e.g., $, %) in graph data, if possible
- To add units on graph, click on graph, right click on data points, and select "Format Data Labels" and go to "Number" tab

More efficient

Breakdown of business unit's sales
% of total sales

E
7%
D 15%
33% A
C 20%
25%
B

Annual sales by product
$ millions

X1 ▭ $50
X2 ▭ $35
X3 ▭ $25
X4 ▯ $10

Formatting Principle—Eye Pleasing:
On tables, bold and right align all column headings

Less efficient

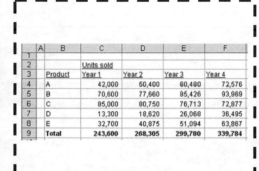

	A	B	C	D	E	F
1						
2			Units sold			
3		Product	Year 1	Year 2	Year 3	Year 4
4		A	42,000	50,400	60,480	72,576
5		B	70,600	77,660	85,426	93,969
6		C	85,000	80,750	76,713	72,877
7		D	13,300	18,620	26,068	36,495
8		E	32,700	40,875	51,094	63,867
9		Total	243,600	268,305	299,780	339,784

Benefits

- Answers the audience's first question about table—"What am I looking at?"
- Easier for audience to see which heading aligns with which data column
- Solid line versus individual underlining is more eye pleasing

More efficient

	A	B	C	D	E	F
1						
2			**Units sold**			
3		**Product**	**Year 1**	**Year 2**	**Year 3**	**Year 4**
4		A	42,000	50,400	60,480	72,576
5		B	70,600	77,660	85,426	93,969
6		C	85,000	80,750	76,713	72,877
7		D	13,300	18,620	26,068	36,495
8		E	32,700	40,875	51,094	63,867
9		**Total**	**243,600**	**268,305**	**299,780**	**339,784**

Ways to improve

- On tables, bold all column headings
- Use line to separate headings from data but do not use underline font style (Ctrl+U); instead, use a horizontal line in PowerPoint or a "Bottom Border" in Excel:

- Also, right align column headings (rather than left or center aligned) since data is automatically right aligned in Excel

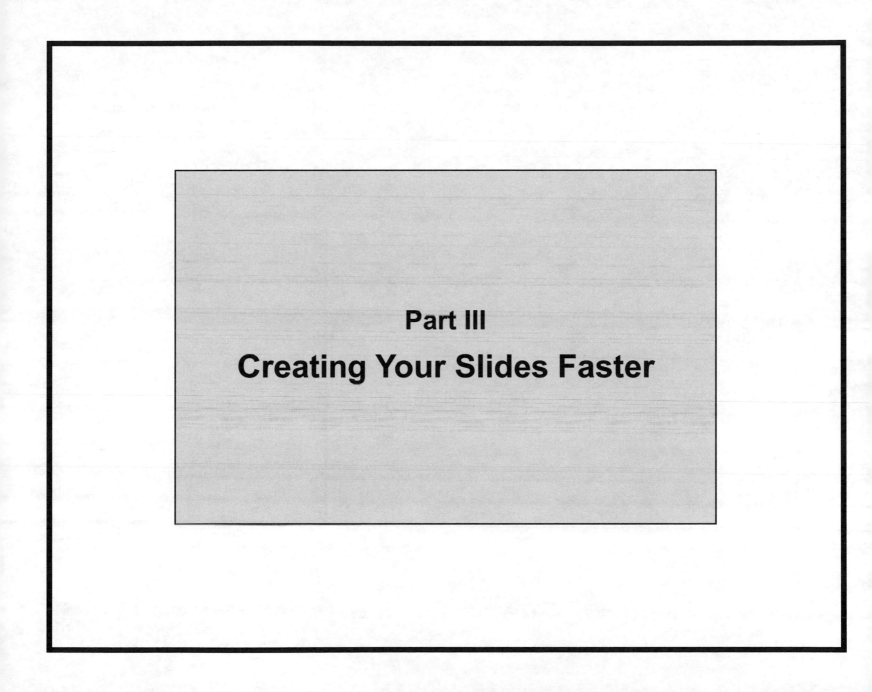

Chapter 9 Speed Tips to Create Slides Faster

Simple techniques to plan, design, and deliver presentations that get results

Part III explains how you can accomplish all of this and still be home in time for dinner by using PowerPoint speed tips and "Quick Hit FAQs." The first recommendation is to leverage slides you've already created and reuse them rather than creating slides from scratch every time. The rest of Chapter 9 details instructions on finding and using speed toolbars and shortcuts, such as aligning text boxes and copying and pasting shapes in a way that saves you time.

Do NOT create slides from scratch—reuse previously created slides from old presentations

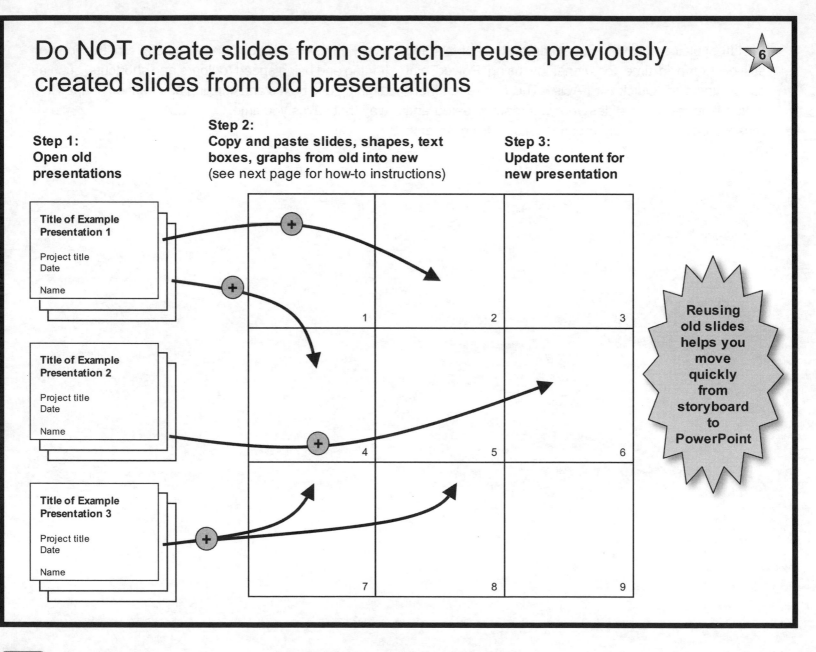

Step 1:
Open old presentations

Step 2:
Copy and paste slides, shapes, text boxes, graphs from old into new
(see next page for how-to instructions)

Step 3:
Update content for new presentation

Title of Example Presentation 1

Project title
Date

Name

Title of Example Presentation 2

Project title
Date

Name

Title of Example Presentation 3

Project title
Date

Name

1

2

3

4

5

6

7

8

9

Reusing old slides helps you move quickly from storyboard to PowerPoint

Instructions for copying and pasting a slide from one presentation file to another

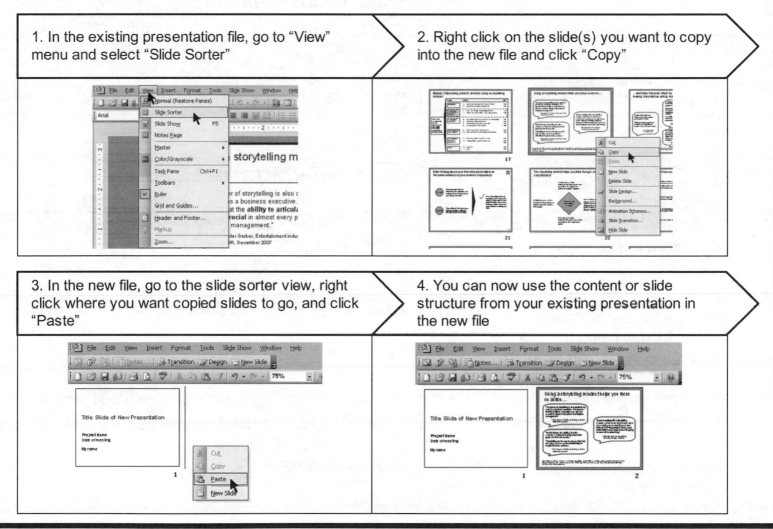

1. In the existing presentation file, go to "View" menu and select "Slide Sorter"

2. Right click on the slide(s) you want to copy into the new file and click "Copy"

3. In the new file, go to the slide sorter view, right click where you want copied slides to go, and click "Paste"

4. You can now use the content or slide structure from your existing presentation in the new file

Take advantage of shortcut "speed" toolbars

Steps to find "speed" toolbars

1. From the menu bar, go to "View" → "Toolbars" → "Drawing"

2. Click on "Draw" from that toolbar and grab the following speed buttons:
   - *"Order"*
   - *"Align or Distribute"*
   - *"Rotate or Flip"*

3. Drag the toolbar box away from the Draw menu by holding the mouse on top of the box (see image below)

4. Then release the toolbar box on your screen

"Speed" toolbar: *ORDER*

"Speed" toolbar: *ALIGN OR DISTRIBUTE*

"Speed" toolbar: *ROTATE OR FLIP*

PowerPoint Presentations That Sell

ILLUSTRATION: "Align" toolbar

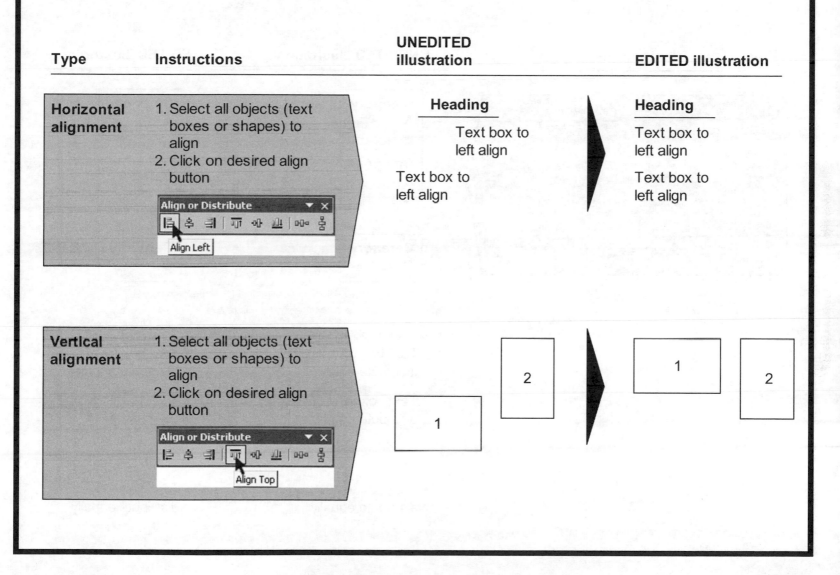

Type	Instructions	UNEDITED illustration	EDITED illustration
Horizontal alignment	1. Select all objects (text boxes or shapes) to align 2. Click on desired align button		
Vertical alignment	1. Select all objects (text boxes or shapes) to align 2. Click on desired align button		

ILLUSTRATION: "Distribute" toolbar

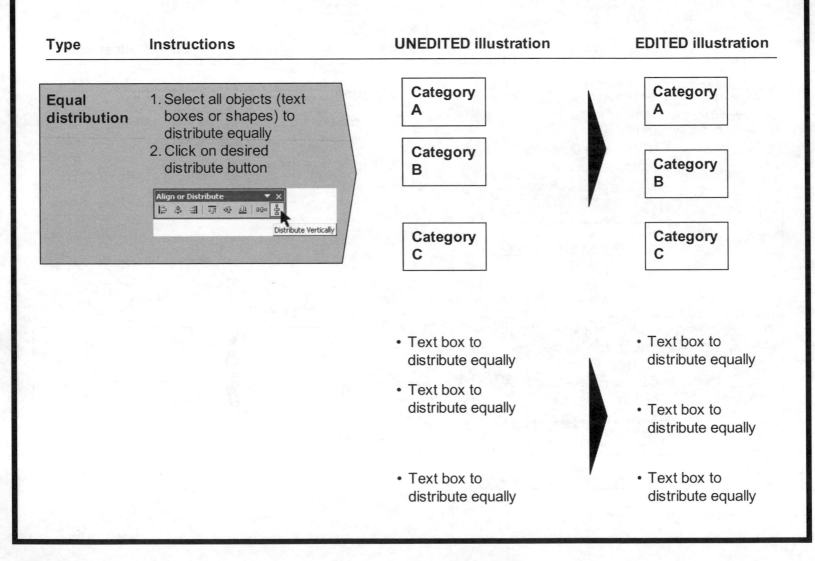

Type	Instructions	UNEDITED illustration	EDITED illustration
Equal distribution	1. Select all objects (text boxes or shapes) to distribute equally 2. Click on desired distribute button	Category A · Category B · Category C	Category A · Category B · Category C

Align or Distribute

Distribute Vertically

- Text box to distribute equally
- Text box to distribute equally
- Text box to distribute equally

- Text box to distribute equally
- Text box to distribute equally
- Text box to distribute equally

Shortcut keyboard tricks to make editing easier:
Moving and copying objects

Desired action	Keyboard strokes to create action	What it will look like on the screen
Move text box, line, or shape while maintaining horizontal or vertical alignment	1. Click and hold down Shift key 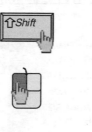 2. Click and hold mouse on object while holding Shift 3. Drag object up/down/left/right 4. Release mouse *before* Shift	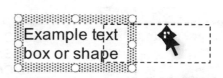 **NOTE:** *Text box moves at same height as current position.*
Copy/duplicate text box, line, or shape while maintaining horizontal or vertical alignment	1. Hold down Ctrl and Shift keys simultaneously 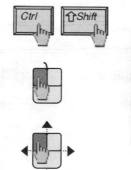 2. Click and hold mouse on object, while holding Ctrl and Shift 3. Drag object up/down/left/right 4. Release mouse before Shift/Ctrl	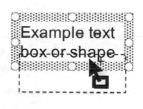 **NOTE:** *New duplicate text box appears with same left alignment as current position.*

Shortcut keyboard tricks to make editing easier:
Horizontal and vertical lines

Desired action	Keyboard strokes to create action	What it will look like on the screen

Create exactly horizontal and vertical straight lines

1. Click "Line" button in AutoShapes (access AutoShapes through the "Drawing" menu, which you can access by clicking on the "View" menu; select "Toolbars," "Drawing")

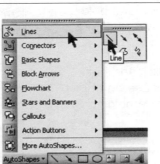 

 First click here   Release mouse here

2. Click and hold down Shift key

3. Click and hold mouse on screen while holding Shift key

4. Drag mouse up/down/left/right

5. Release mouse *before* Shift key

Shortcut keyboard tricks to make editing easier:
Exact circles and squares

Desired action	Keyboard strokes to create action	What it will look like on the screen

Create exact circles and squares

1. Click "Oval" or "Rectangle" button in AutoShapes (access AutoShapes through the "Drawing" menu, which you can access by clicking on the "View" menu; select "Toolbars," "Drawing")

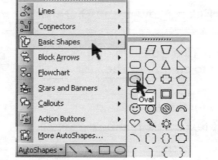

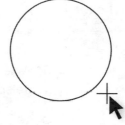

2. Click and hold down Shift key

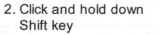

3. Click and hold mouse on screen, while holding Shift

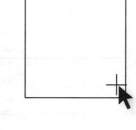

4. Drag mouse to create

5. Release mouse *before* Shift key

Shortcut keyboard tricks to make editing easier: *Reformatting bullets*

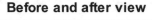

Desired action	Keyboard strokes to create action	Icon	Before and after view

Left align lines of bulleted text within text box	1. Show Ruler: "View" menu → "Ruler"
	
	2. Click on Text Box icon and click on screen to start a text box
	
	3. Write your first line of text
	4. Select text inside text box
	
	5. Click on Bullet icon
	
	6. Separate the little arrows in the Ruler:
	   1. Click mouse on bottom little arrow
	   2. Drag bottom arrow to the right 3–5 notches and release mouse (both arrows will move together to the right)
	   3. Then click mouse on top little arrow
	   4. Drag top arrow to the left the same number of notches and release mouse

			• Sample text to show how to improve bullet alignment
			• Sample text to show how to improve bullet alignment
			
			• Sample text to show how to improve bullet alignment
			• Sample text to show how to improve bullet alignment

Shortcut keyboard tricks to make editing easier:
Reformatting text boxes

Desired action	Keyboard strokes to create action	Before and after view

Format text box to improve look and ability to align multiple text boxes	• Open "Format AutoShape" by right clicking on object and selecting "Format AutoShape"
	
	• Click on "Text Box" tab and adjust the following:
	  – Text anchor point: *Top*
	  – Internal margin: *Set to 0*
	  – Word wrap text in AutoShape: *Check the box*
	  – Resize AutoShape to fit text: *Check the box*
		This is a sample text box
		
		This is a sample text box

Format AutoShape ☒

| Colors and Lines | Size | Position | Picture | Text Box | Web |

Text anchor point: [Top]

Internal margin

Left: [0"]   Top: [0"]

Right: [0"]   Bottom: [0"]

☑ Word wrap text in AutoShape
☑ Resize AutoShape to fit text
☐ Rotate text within AutoShape by 90°

Chapter 10 Quick Hit FAQs: Answers to Common Questions

Simple techniques to plan, design, and deliver presentations that get results

Chapter 10, "Quick Hit FAQs: Answers to Common Questions," provides step-by-step instructions with corresponding visualizations for over 25 topics to help you execute the book's recommendations.

"Quick Hit FAQs"—Use this section to become more efficient

Description

- "Quick Hit FAQs" help you handle some of the more frequently asked questions about creating and editing slides and presentations

- Refer back to this list for step-by-step illustrations to become more efficient at creating presentations that sell

Category	How do I...	Page
Create/edit text box	• Create a text box? Format a text box?	151
	• Change size of text box and alignment of text?	152
	• Change the font, size, style, and color of text?	153
	• Create a text box with bullets?	154
	• Change the type of bullet used in a text box?	155
	• Make the words inside a bulleted text box line up?	156
	• Wrap the text to the next line in a text box?	157
	• Change the line spacing in a text box?	158
	• Quickly duplicate (copy and paste) text boxes?	159
	• Align multiple text boxes next to each other?	160
	• Equally space out text boxes?	161
Create/edit line or shape	• Create a straight line? Rectangle? Other shape?	162
	• Change the background or line color of a shape?	163
	• Format a line to be dotted, thicker, or with arrows?	164
	• Rotate a shape or line?	165
Present on slide	• Present a long list of something?	166
	• Present a timeline of events?	167
	• Present data in a table?	168–169
	• Paste a table from Excel into PowerPoint?	170
	• Paste a graph from Excel into PowerPoint?	171–172
	• Add a footnote or source to the bottom of a slide?	173
	• Choose an appropriate font size for my slides?	174–175
	• Insert an image/picture onto a slide? Change image's size?	176
Edit presentation	• Add a new slide or copy a slide from an existing presentation?	177
	• Reorder slides in my PowerPoint file?	178
	• Change the slide background (i.e., Slide Master)?	179
	• Add or edit slide page numbers?	180
	• Use slide animation?	181

Note: This chapter contains PowerPoint 2003 screenshots in the step-by-step instructions. For those using PowerPoint 2007, look for the corresponding 2007 version of the screenshots in Appendix A.

Quick Hit FAQ: How do I . . .
Create a text box? Format a text box?

Step-by-step instructions	Visualization of key steps

Create a text box

1. Open the "Draw toolbar" if it is not already open by clicking the "View" menu → "Toolbars" → "Drawing"
2. In the Draw toolbar, select "Text Box" icon
3. Then click your mouse on the slide where you want a new text box to be located
4. Type the text you want to appear in the text box

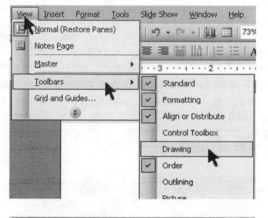

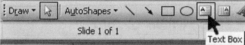

Format a text box

1. Open "Format Text Box" by right clicking on text box and selecting "Format Text Box..." or go to "Format" menu → "Text Box..."
2. In the window that appears, click on the "Text Box" tab and adjust the following:
   – Text anchor point: "Top"
   – Internal margin: Set to "0"
   – Word wrap text in AutoShape: Check the box
   – Resize AutoShape to fit text: Check the box
   Note: This formatting allows you to align multiple text boxes more easily by using the Speed Tips in Part III.

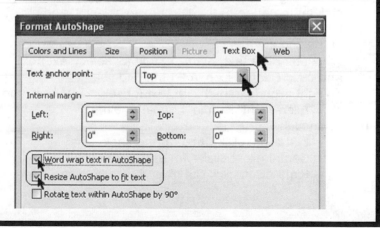

Quick Hit FAQ: How do I . . .
Change size of text box and alignment of text?

Change size of text box

1. Click the mouse on one of the text box's corners to select text box
2. While holding the mouse button down, drag the mouse until the desired text box size is achieved (note: to keep the proportions of the text box constant, hold down Shift while dragging mouse)

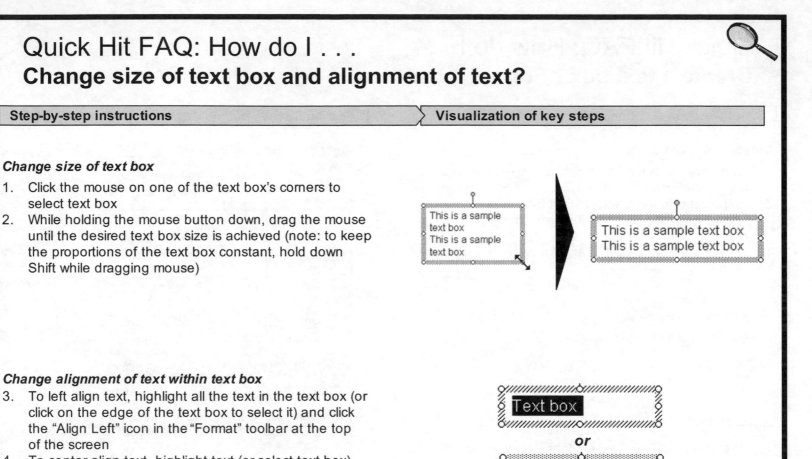

Change alignment of text within text box

3. To left align text, highlight all the text in the text box (or click on the edge of the text box to select it) and click the "Align Left" icon in the "Format" toolbar at the top of the screen
4. To center align text, highlight text (or select text box) and click "Center" icon in "Format" toolbar
5. To right align text, highlight text (or select text box) and click "Align Right" icon in "Format" toolbar
6. Shortcuts:
   - Left align: click Ctrl+L at the same time
   - Center align: click Ctrl+E at the same time
   - Right align: click Ctrl+R at the same time

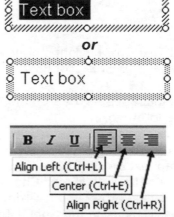

Quick Hit FAQ: How do I . . .
Change the font, size, style, and color of text?

Step-by-step instructions	Visualization of key steps

First, highlight the text or select the text box

1. Highlight the text within the text box by clicking the mouse inside the text box and dragging across all the text or clicking Ctrl+A
2. Alternatively, you can select the entire text box by holding down Shift and clicking once anywhere on the text box(es) you want to change

Change font and size of text

- Once text is highlighted/selected, click on "Format" menu → "Font..." and change "Size" in the box that appears
- Alternatively, select a different text size from the "Font Size" icon in the "Format" toolbar

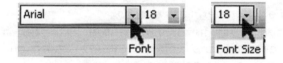

Change style of text (e.g., bold, italics, underline)

- Once text is highlighted/selected, click on "Format" menu → "Font..." and change "Font style" or "Effects" in the box that appears
- Alternatively, select a different text style by using the "Bold," "Italic," or "Underline" icon in the "Format" toolbar
- Shortcut: Bold: click Ctrl+B at the same time
- Shortcut: Italics: click Ctrl+I at the same time
- Shortcut: Underline: click Ctrl+U at the same time

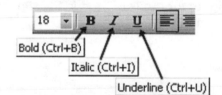

Change color of text

- Once text is highlighted/selected, click on "Format" menu → "Font..." and change "Color" in the box that appears
- Alternatively, select a different text color from the "Font Color" icon in the "Format" toolbar at the top of the screen

Quick Hit FAQ: How do I . . .
Create a text box with bullets?

Create a text box

1. Open the "Draw toolbar" if it is not already open by clicking the "View" menu → "Toolbars" → "Drawing"
2. In the "Draw" toolbar, select "Insert Text Box" icon, which will create a new text box on screen
3. Type the text you want to appear in the text box

See p. 151,
"How do I create a text box?"
for visualization

Add bullets/numbering to text box

4. To add bullets/numbering, highlight all the text in the text box and go to the "Format" menu → "Bullets and Numbering" and select which type of bullet you want
5. Alternatively, highlight all the text and click on either the "Numbering" or the "Bullets" icon in the "Format" toolbar at the top of the screen

Note: See next set of pages for step-by-step instructions for editing bulleted text boxes.

PowerPoint Presentations That Sell

Quick Hit FAQ: How do I . . .
Change the type of bullet used in a text box?

Step-by-step instructions	Visualization of key steps

Create and select text box

1. Create a text box with bullets by using instructions on previous page
2. Highlight the text within the text box by clicking the mouse inside the text box and dragging across all the text or clicking Ctrl+A. Alternatively, you can select the entire text box by holding down Shift and clicking once anywhere on the text box(es) you want to change

Change the type of bullet used in text box

3. To change the type of bullets/numbering, go to the "Format" menu → "Bullets and Numbering"

4. Select which type of bullet or number you desire (to switch between bullets and numbers, use tabs at top of box)
5. You can also select a custom bullet by clicking on the "Customize" button in the "Bulleted" tab
6. Click "OK"

Note: The next page has step-by-step instructions for making words inside a bulleted text box line up.

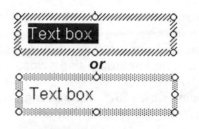

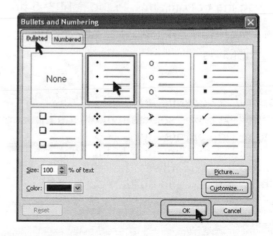

Quick Hit FAQ: How do I . . .
Make the words inside a bulleted text box line up?

Step-by-step instructions	Visualization of key steps

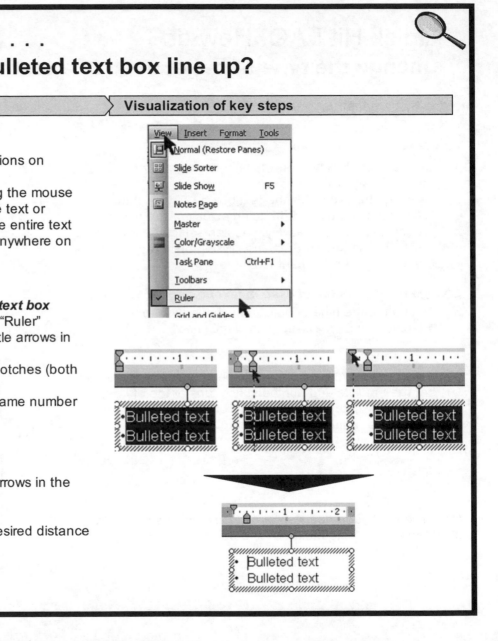

Create and select text box

1. Create a text box with bullets by using instructions on previous pages
2. Highlight the text within the text box by clicking the mouse inside the text box and dragging across all the text or clicking Ctrl+A. Alternatively, you can select the entire text box by holding down Shift and clicking once anywhere on the text box(es) you want to change

Use Ruler to change how the text is lined up in text box

3. Show the ruler by clicking the "View" menu → "Ruler"
4. Once the text box is selected, separate the little arrows in the Ruler:
   - Drag the bottom arrow to the right 3–5 notches (both arrows will move together to the right)
   - Then drag the top arrow to the left the same number of notches

Change distance between text and bullets

5. Once the text box is selected, move the miniarrows in the Ruler to realign bulleted text
   - Drag the bottom arrow to the right
   - Drag the top arrow to the left until the desired distance between text and bullet is achieved

Quick Hit FAQ: How do I . . .
Wrap the text to the next line in a text box?

First, create text box and select text

1. Create a text box with or without bullets by using instructions on previous pages
2. Highlight the text within the text box by clicking the mouse inside the text box and dragging across all the text or clicking Ctrl+A. Alternatively, you can select the entire text box by holding down Shift and clicking once anywhere on the text box(es) you want to change

Wrap the text by reformatting text box

3. Open "Format Text Box" by right clicking on the text box and selecting "Format Text Box..." or go to "Format" menu → "Text Box..."
4. In the window that appears, click on the "Text Box" tab and adjust the following:
   - Text anchor point: "Top"
   - Internal margin: Set to "0"
   - Word wrap text in AutoShape: Check the box
   - Resize AutoShape to fit text: Check the box

Note: This formatting allows you to align multiple text boxes more easily by using the Speed Tips in Part III.

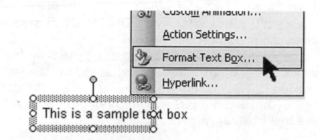

Quick Hit FAQ: How do I . . .
Change the line spacing in a text box?

First, create text box and select text

1. Create a text box with or without bullets by using instructions on previous pages
2. Highlight the text within the text box by clicking the mouse inside the text box and dragging across all the text or clicking Ctrl+A. Alternatively, you can select the entire text box by holding down Shift and clicking once anywhere on the text box(es) you want to change

Change the line spacing

3. Note: increasing the line spacing between text lines can make the slide more readable
4. Go to "Format" menu → "Line Spacing…"
5. In the window that appears:
   - "Line spacing" increases or decreases the space between each line of text
   - "Before paragraph" increases the space just above a line of text after a carriage return (i.e., after you hit "Enter" in the text box)
   - "After paragraph" increases the space just below a line of text after a carriage return (i.e., after you hit "Enter" in the text box)
   - Hit OK once changes are made

   Note: "After paragraph" option (set at 0.2–0.4 lines) is most commonly used because it only adds space between complete bullets rather than using "Line spacing," which adds space between *each* line within a bullet.

Line Spacing

Line spacing
| 1 | ⇕ | Lines |

Before paragraph
| 0 | ⇕ | Lines |

After paragraph
| 0.3 | ⇕ | Lines |

OK   Cancel   Preview

X *Line spacing: 1.3*
After paragraph: 0

- Bulleted text box to show line spacing differences
- Bulleted text box to show line spacing differences
- Bulleted text box to show line spacing differences

✓ *Line spacing: 1*
After paragraph: 0.3

- Bulleted text box to show line spacing differences
- Bulleted text box to show line spacing differences
- Bulleted text box to show line spacing differences

Quick Hit FAQ: How do I . . .
Quickly duplicate (copy and paste) text boxes?

Step-by-step instructions	Visualization of key steps

First, select text box

1. Select each text box/object you want to duplicate by holding down Shift and clicking once anywhere on each text box/object (remember to keep holding down Shift until all text boxes/objects are selected)

Quickly duplicate (copy and paste) text box

- Use Ctrl and Shift keys to quickly duplicate and maintain alignment of text boxes or objects
- Hold down Ctrl and Shift simultaneously
- Click and hold mouse on text box/object while holding Ctrl and Shift
- Drag object up/down/left/right
- Release mouse before releasing Ctrl/Shift
- Note: This is a great timesaving tip that you should use on most slides you create

NOTE: New duplicate text box appears with same left/top alignment as current position

Quickly move text box (without duplicating)

- Use Shift key to quickly move and maintain alignment of text boxes or objects
- Click and hold down Shift key
- Click and hold mouse on object while holding Shift
- Drag object up/down/left/right
- Release mouse before releasing Shift
- Note: This is a great timesaving tip that prevents you from having to realign text boxes/objects once moved

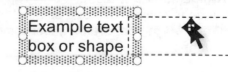

NOTE: Text box moves at same height as current position

Quick Hit FAQ: How do I . . .
Align multiple text boxes next to each other?

| Step-by-step instructions | Visualization of key steps |

First, open the "Align or Distribute" toolbar

1. Open the "Drawing" toolbar from "View" menu →
   "Toolbars" → "Drawing" if it is not currently open
2. Click on "Draw" from that toolbar and grab the "Align or
   Distribute" toolbar (see visualization on the top right)
3. Drag the toolbar box away from the "Draw" menu by
   holding mouse on top of the box
4. Then release the toolbar box on the screen by releasing
   the mouse

Select text boxes

5. Select each text box/object you want to align by holding
   down Shift and clicking once anywhere on each text
   box/object (remember to keep holding down Shift until all
   text boxes/objects are selected)

Align text boxes

6. Once the boxes/objects have been selected, click the
   mouse on the "Align Left," "Align Right," "Align Top," or
   "Align Bottom" button from the "Align or Distribute" toolbar
7. Note: "Align Left" and "Align Top" are the most commonly
   used alignment buttons

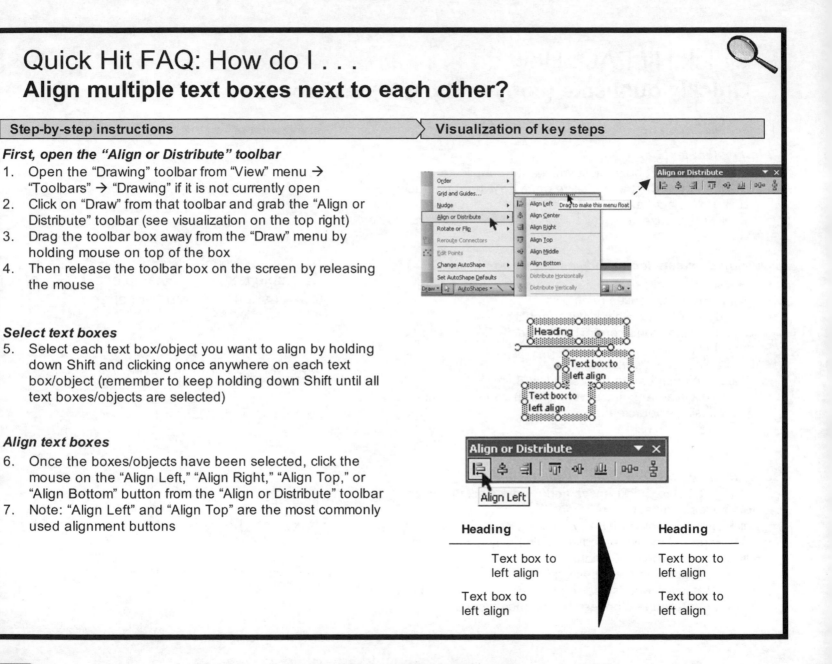

Quick Hit FAQ: How do I . . .
Equally space out text boxes?

Step-by-step instructions	Visualization of key steps

First, open the "Align or Distribute" toolbar

1. Open the "Drawing" toolbar from "View" menu →
   "Toolbars" → "Drawing" if it is not currently open
2. Click on "Draw" from that toolbar and grab the "Align or
   Distribute" toolbar (see visualization on the top right)
3. Drag the toolbar box away from the "Draw" menu by
   holding mouse on top of the box
4. Then release the toolbar box on the screen by releasing
   the mouse

Select text boxes

5. Select each text box/object you want to align by holding
   down Shift and clicking once anywhere on each text
   box/object (remember to keep holding down Shift until all
   text boxes/objects are selected)

Equally space out text boxes

6. Once the boxes/objects have been selected, click the
   mouse on the "Distribute Horizontally" or "Distribute
   Vertically" button from the "Align or Distribute" toolbar
7. Note: "Distribute Vertically" is the most commonly used
   distribute button

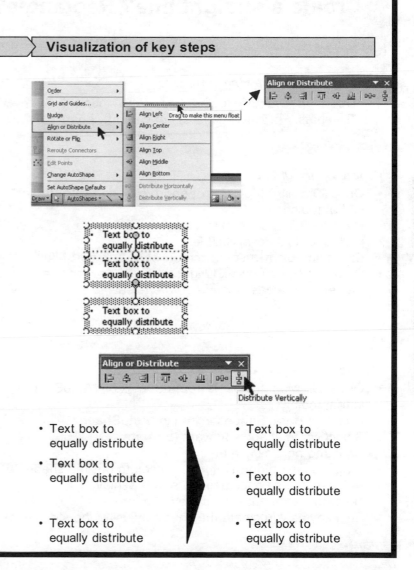

Quick Hit FAQ: How do I . . .
Create a straight line? Rectangle? Other shape?

Step-by-step instructions	Visualization of key steps

First, open the "Drawing" toolbar

1. Open the "Drawing" toolbar from "View" menu →
   "Toolbars" → "Drawing" if it is not currently open

Create a straight line

- Once "Drawing" toolbar is opened, click on "AutoShapes" in that toolbar
- Click the "Lines" button in "AutoShapes" menu
- Click and hold down Shift key
- Click and hold mouse on screen while holding Shift
- Drag mouse up/down/left/right to create desired line
- Remember: release mouse *before* releasing the Shift key

Create a rectangle or other shape

- Once "Drawing" toolbar is opened, click on "AutoShapes" in that toolbar
- Click the "Basic Shapes" menu in "AutoShapes"
- Select which shape you want to create
- Click and hold mouse on screen
- Drag mouse up/down/left/right to create desired shape
- Release mouse once desired size is achieved
- Note: to create an exact circle or square, hold down the Shift key as you create the shape by using the steps above

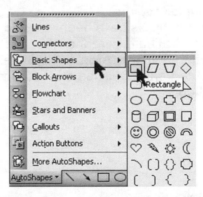

PowerPoint Presentations That Sell

Quick Hit FAQ: How do I . . .
Change the background or line color of a shape?

Step-by-step instructions	Visualization of key steps

Open "Drawing" toolbar and select shape(s)

1. Open the "Drawing" toolbar from "View" menu →
   "Toolbars" → "Drawing" if it is not currently open
2. Select each shape you want to edit by holding down Shift
   and clicking once anywhere on each shape (remember to
   keep holding down Shift until all shapes are selected)

Change background color of shape

- Once shape(s) is selected, click on "Fill Color" button in
  the "Drawing" toolbar (click on the little arrow next to paint
  bucket) and select desired color
- You can access additional colors by clicking on "More Fill
  Colors..."

Change line color of shape

- Once shape(s) is selected, click on "Line Color" button in
  the "Drawing" toolbar (click on the little arrow next to
  paintbrush) and select desired color
- You can access additional colors by clicking on "More Line
  Colors..."

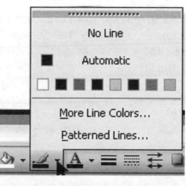

Quick Hit FAQ: How do I . . .
Format a line to be dotted, thicker, or with arrows?

| Step-by-step instructions | Visualization of key steps |

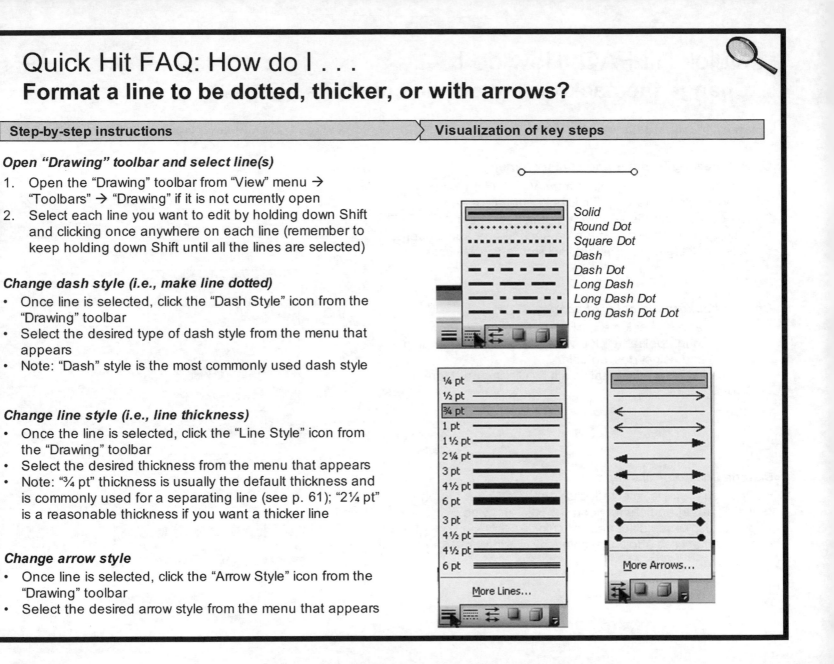

Open "Drawing" toolbar and select line(s)

1. Open the "Drawing" toolbar from "View" menu → "Toolbars" → "Drawing" if it is not currently open
2. Select each line you want to edit by holding down Shift and clicking once anywhere on each line (remember to keep holding down Shift until all the lines are selected)

Change dash style (i.e., make line dotted)

- Once line is selected, click the "Dash Style" icon from the "Drawing" toolbar
- Select the desired type of dash style from the menu that appears
- Note: "Dash" style is the most commonly used dash style

Change line style (i.e., line thickness)

- Once the line is selected, click the "Line Style" icon from the "Drawing" toolbar
- Select the desired thickness from the menu that appears
- Note: "¾ pt" thickness is usually the default thickness and is commonly used for a separating line (see p. 61); "2¼ pt" is a reasonable thickness if you want a thicker line

Change arrow style

- Once line is selected, click the "Arrow Style" icon from the "Drawing" toolbar
- Select the desired arrow style from the menu that appears

Quick Hit FAQ: How do I . . .
Rotate a shape or line?

Step-by-step instructions	Visualization of key steps

First, open the "Rotate or Flip" toolbar

1. Open the "Drawing" toolbar from "View" menu →
   "Toolbars" → "Drawing" if it is not currently open
2. Click on "Draw" from that toolbar and grab the "Rotate or
   Flip" toolbar (see visualization on the top right)
3. Drag the toolbar box away from the "Draw" menu by
   holding the mouse on top of the box
4. Then release the toolbar box on your screen by releasing
   the mouse

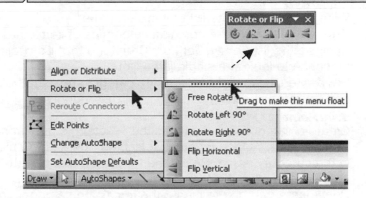

Select shape or line

5. Select each shape or line you want to rotate by holding
   down Shift and clicking once anywhere on each
   shape/line (remember to keep holding down Shift until all
   the shapes/lines are selected)

Rotate shape or line

6. Once the shapes or lines have been selected, click the
   mouse on the "Rotate Left 90°" or "Rotate Right 90°"
   button from the "Rotate or Flip" toolbar
7. Note: you can also use the green dot above the selected
   text box to rotate, but the 90° rotation and horizontal and
   vertical flips are the most commonly used

Before rotation   *After rotation*

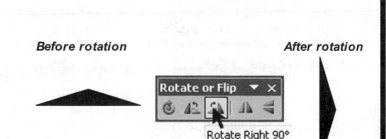

Rotate Right 90°

Quick Hit FAQ: How do I . . .
Present a long list of something?

Step-by-step instructions	Visualization of key steps

Before PowerPoint

1. Write out the complete list of items on paper
2. Within the list, find 2–4 common categories of items that you can use to divide the list (remember from Chapter 5 that it's challenging for the audience to look at a single large list)
3. Handwrite storyboard of slide with "category boxes," "bold headings," and "bulleted text boxes" (see visualization on right)

In PowerPoint

4. Create a category box by using the "Rectangle" tool from "AutoShapes."* Once created, select the box with the mouse and type in the category name. Select the text and click Ctrl+B to make it bold
5. Left and top align the text within the rectangle*
6. Copy/paste that box to create the remaining category boxes by holding down Ctrl and Shift keys while dragging box down the slide*
7. Create the bold heading by using "Insert text box" from the "Draw" menu.* Type the word(s) into the text box (e.g., "Description"). Select the text and click Ctrl+B to make it bold
8. Create a horizontal line under the bold heading by using the "Line" tool from "AutoShapes."* Hold the Shift button while dragging the line across the slide to keep it horizontal
9. Create a text box* underneath the bold heading
10. Make it a bulleted text box by selecting the text box and going to the "Format" menu and clicking "Bullets and Numbering…"*
11. Type the list of items for the first category box in the bulleted text box
12. Copy/paste that text box to create the remaining bulleted text boxes for each category box—create a separate text box for every category box
13. If you want to add another level of detail for each item on your list (e.g., "Timing"), create a second column of bold heading and bulleted text boxes by repeating steps 7–12

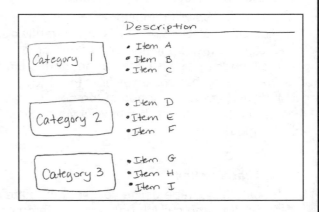

*Refer to the Quick Hit FAQ table of contents at the beginning of this chapter for the pages that describe how to create and edit shapes, lines, and text boxes.

Quick Hit FAQ: How do I . . .
Present a timeline of events?

Step-by-step instructions	Visualization of key steps

Before PowerPoint

1. Situation: You want to illustrate the expected timing of a set of events or activities you're working on and some details for each event
2. Determine 2–4 major events that encompass the entire timeline
3. Handwrite storyboard of slide with arrows across the top with timing and additional details below

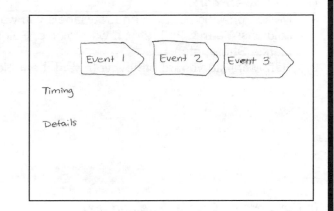

In PowerPoint

4. Create an arrow by using the "Pentagon" or "Chevron" tool from "AutoShapes."* Once created, select the arrow with the mouse and type in the event name. Select the text and click Ctrl+B to make it bold
5. Left align the text within the pentagon or chevron*
6. Copy/paste that shape to the right to create the remaining arrows by holding down Ctrl and Shift keys while dragging shape across the slide*
7. Create the labels for "Timing" and "Details" by using "Insert text box" from the "Draw" menu.* Type the word(s) into the text box. Select the text and click Ctrl+B to make it bold
8. Create a bulleted text box* underneath the arrows
9. Type the list of items in the bulleted text box
10. Copy/paste that bulleted text box to create the remaining bulleted text boxes—create a separate bulleted text box for each part of the slide

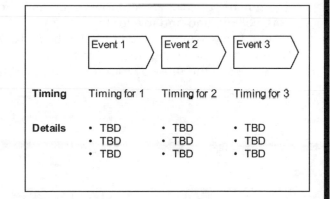

*Refer to the Quick Hit FAQ table of contents at the beginning of this chapter for pages that describe how to create and edit shapes, lines, and text boxes.

Quick Hit FAQ: How do I . . .
Present data in a table?

| Step-by-step instructions | Visualization of key steps |

Before PowerPoint

1. Decide on which column and row labels you want to use (e.g., columns: Year 1, 2, 3, etc.; rows: Volume, Sales, Costs, Profit, Market Share, etc.)
2. Handwrite storyboard of how you want the table to look

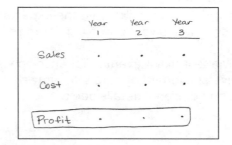

In PowerPoint: Create table and text

3. Create a table by going to the "Insert" menu → "Table . . ." and type the number of columns and rows you desire (remember to include one column and one row for the labels)
4. Alternatively, you can create a table by clicking on the "Insert Table" icon in the "Formatting" toolbar at the top of the screen
5. Insert text in the table by clicking in a cell of the table and type

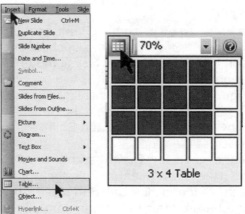

(Continued on next page)

	Year 1	Year 2	Year 3
Sales	100	110	120
Cost	70	75	80
Profit	30	35	40

PowerPoint Presentations That Sell

Quick Hit FAQ: How do I . . .
Present data in a table? (Continued)

In PowerPoint: Format text to maximize impact
(see Chapter 8 in Part II for more formatting principles)

6. Right align data columns by highlighting data columns with mouse and clicking "Align Right" icon in "Formatting" toolbar at top of screen or holding Ctrl+R

7. Remove all borders in table by highlighting all rows and columns, right click in table → "Borders and Fill . . ." option; in the "Borders" tab, click on each of the horizontal and vertical line borders until all the borders are removed; hit OK (see visualization at top right)

8. Format top row of table:
   - Highlight just the top row in the table by selecting the text in the top row with the mouse
   - Right click on the selected top row → "Borders and Fill . . ." option
   - In the "Borders" tab, click the bottom border line only
   - In the "Text Box" tab, change "Text alignment" to "Bottom"
   - Hit OK

9. Bold row and column labels by highlighting text with mouse and clicking Ctrl+B

10. Resize table as desired by selecting entire table (hold down Shift key and click anywhere on table) and then put the mouse in a corner of the table, left click mouse, and drag while holding mouse button down

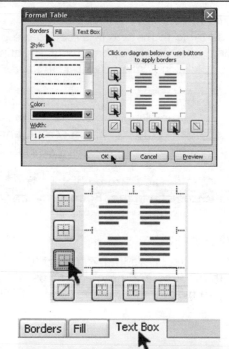

	Year 1	Year 2	Year 3
Sales	100	110	120
Cost	70	75	80
Profit	30	35	40

Quick Hit FAQ: How do I . . .
Paste a table from Excel into PowerPoint?

Format cells in Excel

1. Note: Edit table formatting in Excel before pasting into PowerPoint
2. Right align data column labels by highlighting column cells with mouse and clicking "Align Right" icon (Note: Ctrl+R does not work in Excel)
3. Add bottom border line to the first row of labels by highlighting just the first row and clicking the "Borders" drop-down menu from the "Format" toolbar at the top of the screen and select "Bottom Border"
4. Bold the column and row labels by clicking Ctrl+B once cells are highlighted
5. Resize font to desired size by highlighting all cells and clicking on the "Font Size" icon in the "Format" toolbar at the top of the screen

	A	B	C	D
1		Year 1	Year 2	Year 3
2	Sales	100	110	120
3	Cost	70	75	80
4	Profit	30	35	40

Copy cells in Excel

6. Highlight all Excel cells that you want to paste into PowerPoint by clicking the mouse and dragging across all desired cells
7. Copy these highlighted cells by clicking Ctrl+C

	A	B	C	D
1		Year 1	Year 2	Year 3
2	Sales	100	110	120
3	Cost	70	75	80
4	Profit	30	35	40

Paste into PowerPoint and resize as desired

8. Paste Excel table in PowerPoint by clicking Ctrl+V. Alternatively, you can paste the cells as an image to not allow editing by going to "Edit" → "Paste Special..." → "Picture (Windows Metafile)" and hit OK
9. Resize table by selecting table and clicking mouse on one of the table's corners and dragging to desired size (holding down Shift while dragging maintains table's proportions and prevents the numbers from looking distorted)

	Year 1	Year 2	Year 3
Sales	100	110	120
Cost	70	75	80
Profit	30	35	40

Quick Hit FAQ: How do I . . .
Paste a graph from Excel into PowerPoint?

Format graph in Excel

1. Reformat graph in Excel first to make it presentation-ready by removing unnecessary color and lines by using the following steps:

   A. Remove *y*-axis: Right click on axis → "Clear"
   B. Add values to bars: Right click on bars, "Format Data Series" → "Data Labels" → check "Value"
   C. Recolor bars white: Right click on bars, "Format Data Series" → "Patterns" → make "Area" white
   D. Remove gridlines: Right click on gridlines → "Clear"
   E. Remove legend: Right click on legend → "Clear"
   F. Recolor background: Right click on gray background, "Format Plot Area" → "Patterns" → Border: click "None"; Area: click "None"
   G. Remove outside border color: Right click on black outline of graph, "Format Chart Area" → "Patterns" → Border: click "None"

(Continued on next page)

Unformatted Excel graph

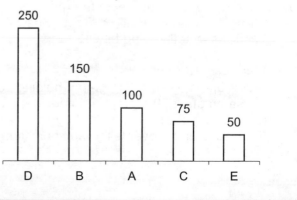

Reformatted Excel graph

Quick Hit FAQ: How do I . . .
Paste a graph from Excel into PowerPoint? (Continued)

Step-by-step instructions	Visualization of key steps

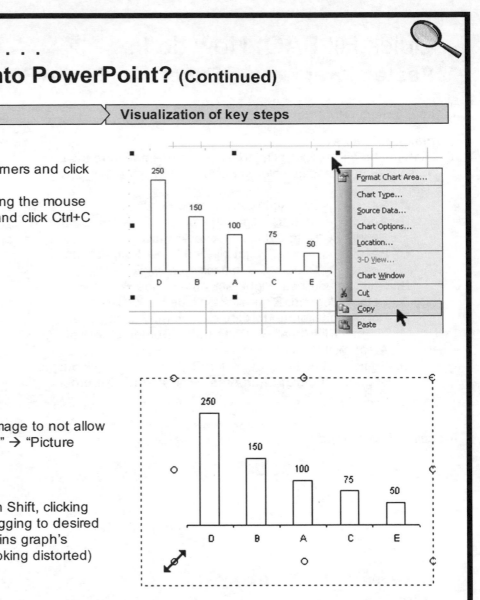

Copy graph in Excel

2. Right click the mouse on one of the graph's corners and click "Copy"
3. Alternatively, you can select the graph by clicking the mouse near one of the corners of the graph in Excel and click Ctrl+C to copy

Paste into PowerPoint and resize as desired

4. Paste graph into PowerPoint by clicking Ctrl+V
5. Alternatively, you can paste the graph as an image to not allow editing by going to "Edit" → "Paste Special . . ." → "Picture (Windows Metafile)" and hit OK

6. Resize graph by selecting graph, holding down Shift, clicking mouse on one of the graph's corners, and dragging to desired size (holding down Shift while dragging maintains graph's proportions and prevents the numbers from looking distorted)

Quick Hit FAQ: How do I . . .
Add a footnote or source to the bottom of a slide?

Step-by-step instructions	Visualization of key steps

Create a text box

1. Open the "Draw" toolbar if it is not already open by clicking the "View" menu → "Toolbars" → "Drawing"
2. In the "Draw" toolbar, click "Insert Text Box" icon
3. Then click the mouse on the slide where you want a new text box to be located
4. Type the text you want to appear in the text box
   - Start text with the word "Source:" or "*"
   - For a source, try to include the date of the source at the end
   - Make font size of source/footnote 1–2 sizes smaller than the font size on the rest of the slide (do not go below font size 9pt for the source/footnote)

Move text box to bottom of screen

5. Select entire source/footnote text box
6. Click mouse on top of selected text box and hold mouse button down
7. Drag text box to bottom left of the slide

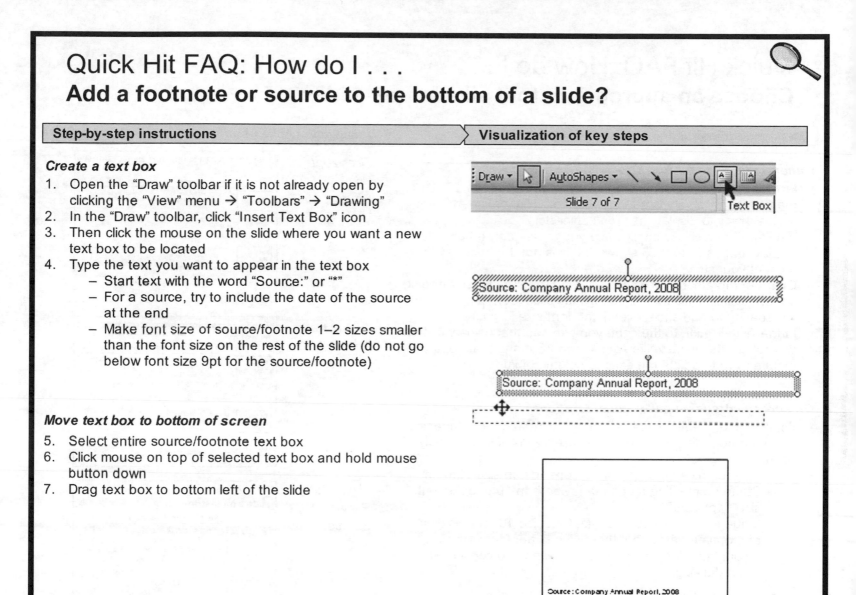

Quick Hit FAQ: How do I . . .
Choose an appropriate font size for my slides?

Step-by-step instructions	Visualization of key steps

General guidance for font size

- From the author's experience at selling ideas through presentations, a very large font size (i.e., 18pt or larger) is not the best way to display the slide's mini-story
- Very large font sizes usually force you to use only a bullet/dash display, but as Chapter 5 showed, this is not the best way to present your story
- Consider the amount of white space on the slide when deciding on font size—more white space makes slide look less intimidating to audience, even if the font size is smaller
- In the visualization to the right, you can see that primary content at 14pt creates more white space than 16pt and that 18pt requires you to delete the second column of information

On-screen versus on-paper considerations

- For on-paper meetings (i.e., slides are printed out on paper and there are no projected slides), font size 12–14pt is commonly used
- For on-screen meetings, guidance depends on size of room:
  - Standard meeting room with fewer than 10 people, font size 14pt is sufficient
  - Large rooms with 20+ people, font size 16–18pt is more appropriate (remember that using larger fonts limits the amount of information you can present, so consider this when drawing your storyboards)

(Continued on next page)

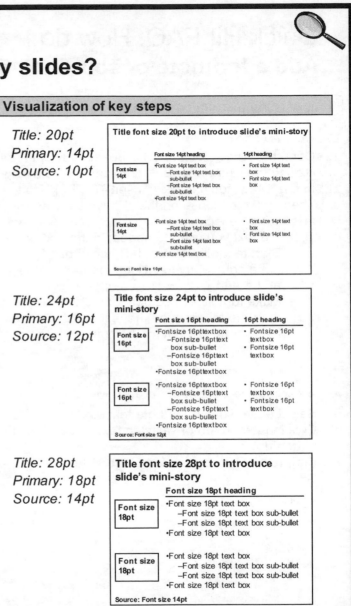

Title: 20pt
Primary: 14pt
Source: 10pt

Title: 24pt
Primary: 16pt
Source: 12pt

Title: 28pt
Primary: 18pt
Source: 14pt

Quick Hit FAQ: How do I . . .
Choose an appropriate font size for my slides? (Continued)

Step-by-step instructions	Visualization of key steps

Primary content font size guidance

- Use the same font size for all primary content (i.e., do not make one text box size 14pt and the other 12pt)
- Commonly used font size for primary content is 14pt (note: Arial font is easy to read at this font size)
- Font size 12pt is okay, but 10pt is small, so try to avoid
- Font size 16pt can be used for simpler slides with less content
- Varying the primary content's font size from slide to slide is okay if necessary

Slide title font size guidance

- Title font size should be a few sizes larger than the primary content to make it stand out more
- Commonly used font size for slide's title is 20–28pt
- Do not make title font so large that you can't fit more than a few words (remember to follow title guidance at beginning of Chapter 6)
- Note: it is okay for slide title to be two lines

Source/footnote font size guidance

- Font size of source/footnote should be 1–2 sizes smaller than the font size of the primary content
- Commonly used font size is 10pt for the source/footnote

Change font and size of text

- Once text is highlighted/selected, click on "Format" menu → "Font..." and change "Size" in the box that appears
- Alternatively, select a different text size from the "Font Size" icon in the "Format" toolbar

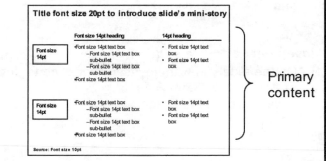

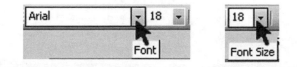

Quick Hit FAQ: How do I . . .
Insert an image/picture onto a slide? Change image's size?

Step-by-step instructions	Visualization of key steps

Save image file on your computer

- Copy/save image file(s) (e.g., files with extensions .jpg, .gif, .tif, etc.) in the folder where your PowerPoint presentation is saved
- Web site images: if you want to use an image from a Web site, you usually can right click on the image in the site and click "Save image as"*

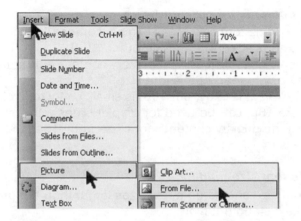

Insert image on to a slide

- On the slide you want to insert image, go to "Insert" menu → "Picture" → "From File . . ."
- Locate your saved image
- Hit "Insert"

Change size of image

- Select image by clicking on it once
- Hold down Shift and click mouse on one of the corners of the selected image and drag the mouse until you have the desired image size
- Note: holding down Shift while dragging maintains the image's current proportions, which prevents the resulting image from looking distorted

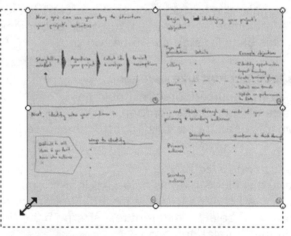

*Remember to check ownership rights of any image from a third party to protect yourself from copyright infringement.

Quick Hit FAQ: How do I . . .
Add a new slide or copy a slide from an existing presentation?

Step-by-step instructions

Visualization of key steps

Insert a new slide

- Go to "Insert" menu → "New Slide"
- Shortcut: click Ctrl+M to insert a new slide

Insert slide from existing presentation

- Option 1: Copy and paste from existing file
  - Open existing presentation file you want to copy from
  - Go to "Slide Sorter View" by going to "View" menu → "Slide Sorter"
  - Select slide(s) you want to copy by clicking and holding Ctrl key, left click on each slide you want, and click Ctrl+C to copy (remember to hold Ctrl down)
  - In the new presentation file, go to Slide Sorter View, click mouse between current slides where you want to insert copied slides, and click Ctrl+V to paste

- Option 2: Use "Insert Slides from Files" function
  - In new presentation, go to "Insert" menu → "Slide from Files . . ."
  - Click "Browse . . ." and open the existing presentation file you want to copy from
  - Select slide(s) you want by left clicking once on each slide (Note: to maintain formatting of existing slides, check "Keep source formatting" box)
  - Hit "Insert"

- Note: Inserting slides from existing presentations is a great way to save time—you don't need to re-create every slide!

Slide Sorter View:

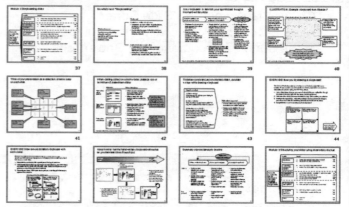

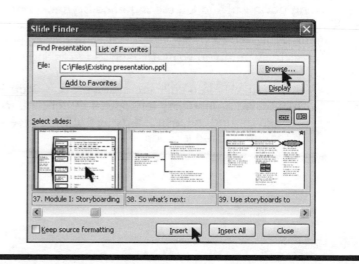

Quick Hit FAQ: How do I . . .
Reorder slides in my PowerPoint file?

Step-by-step instructions	Visualization of key steps

Go to Slide Sorter View

1. Go to "View" menu → "Slide Sorter"
   Alternatively, you can click on the "Slide Sorter View" icon in the bottom left corner of the PowerPoint screen

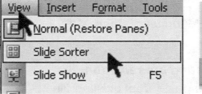

Reorder slides

2. In the Slide Sorter view, select slide(s) you want to move by holding down Ctrl and left clicking once on each slide
3. Once slide(s) are selected, change order by:
   - Clicking Ctrl+X to cut slide(s), clicking mouse between slides where you want to insert, and clicking Ctrl+V to paste
   - Alternatively, drag selected slides around Slide Sorter by clicking and holding left mouse button and moving mouse around; release left mouse button once you have the desired location

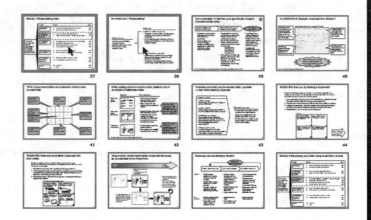

Quick Hit FAQ: How do I . . .
Change the slide background (i.e., Slide Master)?

Step-by-step instructions	Visualization of key steps

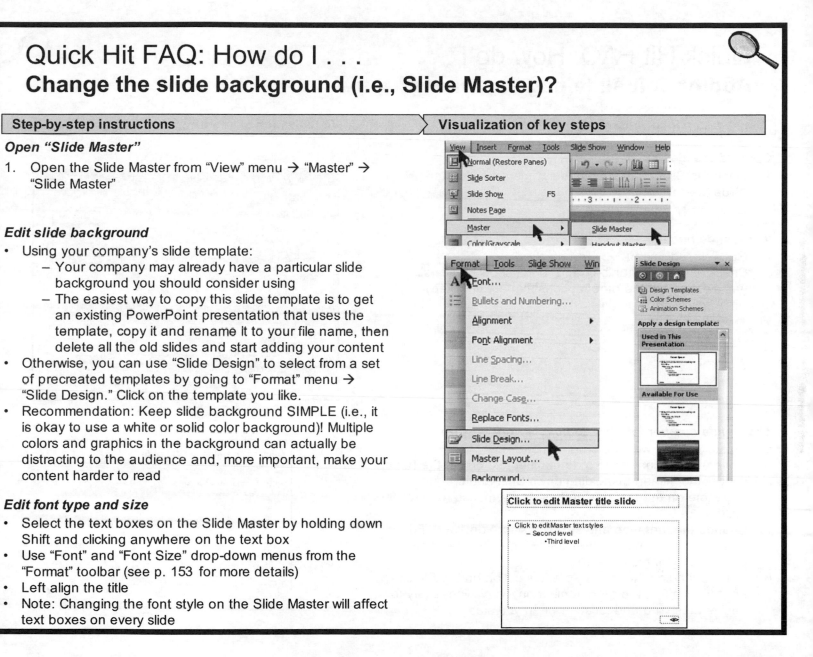

Open "Slide Master"

1. Open the Slide Master from "View" menu → "Master" → "Slide Master"

Edit slide background

- Using your company's slide template:
  - Your company may already have a particular slide background you should consider using
  - The easiest way to copy this slide template is to get an existing PowerPoint presentation that uses the template, copy it and rename It to your file name, then delete all the old slides and start adding your content
- Otherwise, you can use "Slide Design" to select from a set of precreated templates by going to "Format" menu → "Slide Design." Click on the template you like.
- Recommendation: Keep slide background SIMPLE (i.e., it is okay to use a white or solid color background)! Multiple colors and graphics in the background can actually be distracting to the audience and, more important, make your content harder to read

Edit font type and size

- Select the text boxes on the Slide Master by holding down Shift and clicking anywhere on the text box
- Use "Font" and "Font Size" drop-down menus from the "Format" toolbar (see p. 153 for more details)
- Left align the title
- Note: Changing the font style on the Slide Master will affect text boxes on every slide

Quick Hit FAQ: How do I . . .
Add or edit slide page numbers?

Open "Slide Master"

1. Open the Slide Master from "View" menu → "Master" → "Slide Master"

Insert slide number

2. Go to "Insert" menu → "Slide number"
3. Check only "Slide number" and "Don't show on title slide" (unselect any of the other options that are checked)
4. Hit "Apply to All"

Move slide number text box to bottom right of screen

5. Select text box with the slide number
6. Move the location of the slide number text box to the bottom right of the screen by holding down Shift and clicking anywhere on the text box and using the mouse to move the text box
7. Change the font type and size by using "Font" and "Font Size" drop-down menus from the "Format" toolbar (see pp. 174–175 for more details)
8. Note: Changing the font style and location on the Slide Master will affect the slide number on every slide, so try to decide on styling and location when you start

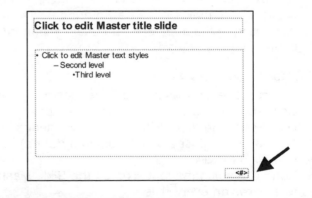

Quick Hit FAQ: How do I . . .
Use slide animation?

General guidance for using animation

- Less animation is better in general:
  - Animation is often more of a distraction than a value-add
  - Audience members can get caught up thinking about the animation you're going to use rather than focusing on the story you're trying to sell
- Some people believe animation keeps the audience entertained, but it usually does not enhance the story and, more important, takes up too much of your time
- Use animation if you *absolutely need* to build out the slide's mini-story in stages
- When using animation, ask yourself, "Does this add to the presentation of my mini-story?" If not, do not spend the time on it
- Animation things to consider:
  - It is okay to not use any animation effects on a particular slide or an entire presentation!
  - For larger meeting rooms (20+ people), animation can help take the audience through the slide
- Animation things to avoid:
  - Any type of sound animation that is not related to the slide's story (these sounds get old after the second slide)
  - Slide transitions that vary between the slides
  - More than 1 or 2 animation effects on a particular slide

Adding animation

1. Go to "Slide Show" menu → "Custom Animation"
2. Select text boxes or shapes you want to animate
3. Click on "Add Effect" drop-down menu
4. Select effect from "Entrance," "Emphasis," "Exit," or "Motion Paths" drop-down menu

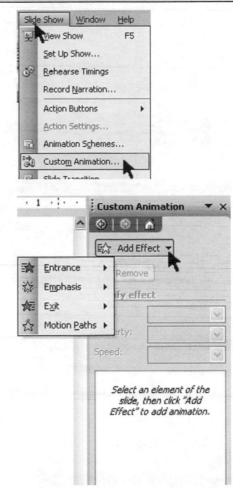

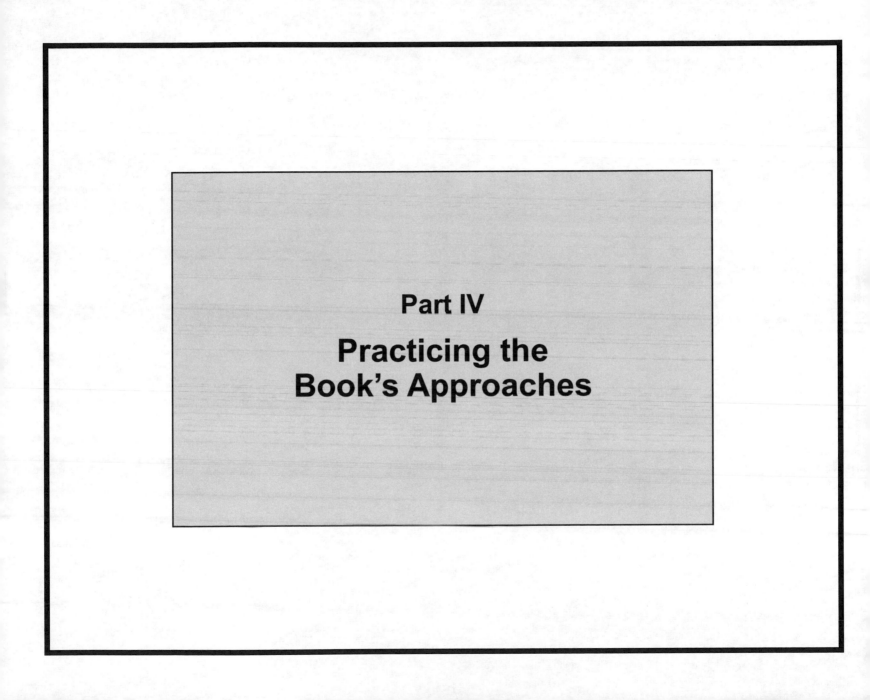

Part IV

Practicing the Book's Approaches

Chapter 11 Case Study: Book's Approach in Action

SImple techniques to plan, design, and deliver presentations that get results

CASE STUDY: Selling your ideas for an internal project: Simulated project for EachMovie company

Background on EachMovie*

- EachMovie is a subscription-based online movie rating service

- Subscribers to the service log in and either rate movies they have seen or look at others' movie ratings

- The data used in this case is a small, representative sample of a large database of movie ratings

- Included in the sample are 80 movies with 2,400 customers' ratings on a scale of 1 to 6 (6 being the best rating):

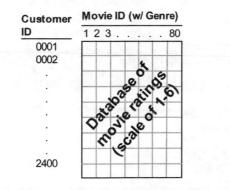

Simulated business situation

You work for EachMovie, and your manager asked you to start a new project with the objective of increasing subscriber use

Goal of this exercise

To show you how to use a storytelling philosophy and smart slide structure to get your ideas initiated

*The EachMovie case is based on a service HP/Compaq Research (formerly DEC Research) operated in the late 1990s. The data used is a sample of actual data from that business before it was shut down.

CASE STUDY: Create a 1-page overview of an "agendicized" project by identifying research areas

More details in Chapter 3

1-slide overview of EachMovie project

Research areas to investigate	Assumed answers	Analyses/data to assess your assumed answers
1. Customers' viewing behavior	• EachMovie should recognize its best customers and target occasional customers to increase viewing frequency	• Distribution of customers by number of movies watched
2. Inventory assessment of movies	• Underperforming movies should be removed from inventory	• Distribution of movies by number of times watched • Distribution of movies by average rating
3. Inventory assessment of genres	• Certain genres may be underperforming and need refreshing	• Rank genres by average views per movie within each genre
4. Benchmark similar content-offering services	• EachMovie can increase viewing frequency by using promotion tactics similar to those used by like services	• Research promotion tactics of similar content providers (e.g., *Wall St. Journal*, Netflix)

Notes

- This page is helpful for showing your manager at the beginning of the project to get agreement on your direction
- You will not necessarily use this slide in the final version of your presentation

CASE STUDY: Before doing your analyses, handwrite storyboard of slides as they may look in PowerPoint

More details in Chapter 4

Notes
- You do not need to write every detail in storyboard—the slide title, a couple of phrases, and the basic slide layout are a helpful start
- Content will require updating once you complete analyses and transition into PowerPoint

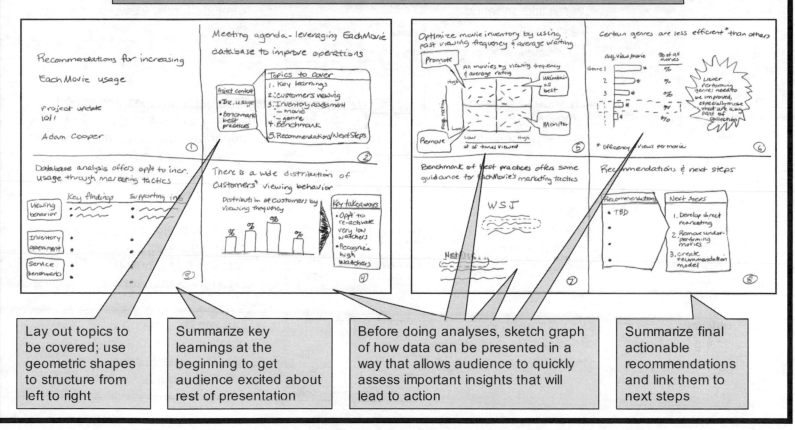

Lay out topics to be covered; use geometric shapes to structure from left to right

Summarize key learnings at the beginning to get audience excited about rest of presentation

Before doing analyses, sketch graph of how data can be presented in a way that allows audience to quickly assess important insights that will lead to action

Summarize final actionable recommendations and link them to next steps

CASE STUDY: Finalize mix of text-driven and data-driven slides

Slide in presentation	Chart type to use	Illustration	Rationale for chart choice See following pages for more details
1. Title page	Simple text with overall title, meeting title and date, author/attendees	**Recommendations for increasing usage** Project update October 1 Adam Cooper	• Title introduces overall story and reminds future viewers of meeting details
2. Context and topics to be covered	Advanced text with geometric shapes separating content	**Topics to cover** **Context** • TBD 1. TBD • TBD 2. TBD 3. TBD	• Geometric shapes are useful when you have two or more separate but related messages to convey on a single slide
3. Summary of key learnings	Bulleted text with geometric shapes to categorize content	**Findings Support** **Viewing behavior** • TBD • TBD • TBD • TBD **Inventory evaluation** • TBD • TBD • TBD • TBD	• Left-to-right format with categories and bold headings makes information more accessible (versus basic bullets and dashes in top-to-bottom format)
4. Customer viewing behavior	Column graph in order of viewing frequency	**Distribution of customers by viewing frequency** % of all customers V.Low Low Med High	• Column graphs are useful for displaying distribution of predetermined groups (i.e., viewing frequency segments)

CASE STUDY: Finalize mix of text-driven and data-driven slides (Continued)

Slide in presentation	Chart type to use	Illustration	Rationale for chart choice See following pages for more details
5. Movie inventory assessment	Scatter graph in a 2×2 matrix with color shading and callout boxes		• 2×2 matrix allows a set of data (e.g., 80 movies) to be compared across two dimensions simultaneously • Callout boxes highlight actionable recommendations
6. Genre inventory assessment	Bar chart in order of largest to smallest with dashed highlight boxes and starburst callout		• Bar charts are useful to rank a set of data (e.g., genres) in order • Highlight boxes draw audience's attention to most important data • Starburst calls out actionable recommendation
7. Benchmark-like services	Images copied from Web site or other promotion material with dashed highlight boxes		• Images/graphics are more impactful than descriptive text • Highlight boxes draw audience's attention to most important detail
8. Recommendations and next steps	Advanced text with geometric shapes separating content		• Geometric shapes are useful when you have two or more separate but related messages to convey on a single slide

CASE STUDY: Create PowerPoint slides by using smart slide structure in Part 2 and speed tips in Part 3

Illustration of book's lessons	Page with details
• Agendicized project of research areas (from one-slide project overview on p. 31) is used directly in meeting topics	30
• Research areas create a path for story to follow	32
• Advanced geometric shapes allow you to deliver two separate but related messages on a single slide	42, 162
• Create trapezoid shape by using "Trapezoid" button in "Basic Shapes" within "AutoShapes" and change fill color to black	

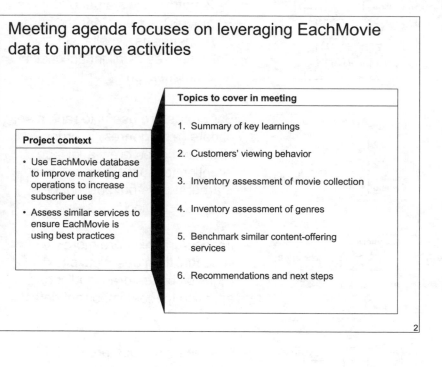

Meeting agenda focuses on leveraging EachMovie data to improve activities

Project context

- Use EachMovie database to improve marketing and operations to increase subscriber use
- Assess similar services to ensure EachMovie is using best practices

Topics to cover in meeting

1. Summary of key learnings
2. Customers' viewing behavior
3. Inventory assessment of movie collection
4. Inventory assessment of genres
5. Benchmark similar content-offering services
6. Recommendations and next steps

PowerPoint Presentations That Sell

CASE STUDY: Create PowerPoint slides (Continued)

EachMovie database analysis offers opportunities to increase use through specific actions

	Opportunities	Supporting information
Viewing behavior	• Majority of subscribers have viewed fewer than 5 movies—opportunity to re-activate one-time viewers through promotion offer • Small group of "movie buffs" can be recognized as best of the best	• 63% of subscribers viewed fewer than 5 movies (21% viewed only 1 movie) • 13% of subscribers viewed 10+ movies
Inventory assessment (movie/genre)	• Opportunity to remove underperforming movies and promote less watched highly rated movies • Drama and Comedy, the two biggest genres in collection, are in the bottom half of viewing efficiency	• ~20% of movies have both low viewing frequency and low rating • Drama and Comedy represent 43% of collection, but average viewing is less than half of top performers
Service benchmarks	• Replicate similar content-offering services that use user viewing/purchasing behavior to make recommendations	• *Wall St. Journal* and Netflix both use marketing language based on users' behavior

Source: EachMovie database; company Web sites.

3

Illustration of book's lessons	Page with details
• Categories in boxes and bold headings in left-to-right format make content more accessible: – Can quickly highlight three areas of findings – Can focus on key findings without going into all the details of the data – Can focus on just one of the areas (e.g., benchmarks)	61, 63
• Considers varying levels of interest across audience by including both high-level findings and supporting data	27–28
• Bulleted text boxes communicate slide's content in an easy-to-read format	63, 154
• Copied and aligned category boxes by using speed tips and toolbars in Part III	159–160

CASE STUDY: Create PowerPoint slides (Continued)

Illustration of book's lessons	Page with details

• Three slide elements—title, learnings, supporting data analysis—introduce, reveal, and support slide's mini-story:
  – Title is meaningful and piques audience's interest
  – Key learnings in shadowed box (plus title) tell enough of an actionable story that audience does not need to look at data
	78–81

• Column chart allows for simple graphical representation of distribution—note that order of series (e.g., segment of movie viewing frequency) is more important than order of bars (e.g., percent of subscribers)	84
• Colored data bars and dashed boxes draw audience's attention to story-vital information	114, 116
• Answers relevant audience data slide questions, and graph is formatted to maximize impact	103

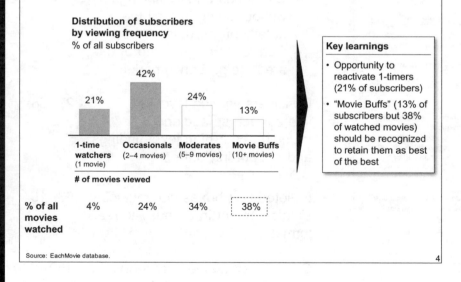

Majority (63%) of subscribers viewed fewer than 5 movies whereas 13% are "Movie Buffs"

Distribution of subscribers by viewing frequency
% of all subscribers

42%

21%

24%

13%

| | 1-time watchers (1 movie) | Occasionals (2–4 movies) | Moderates (5–9 movies) | Movie Buffs (10+ movies) |

# of movies viewed

% of all movies watched: 4% 24% 34% 38%

Key learnings
• Opportunity to reactivate 1-timers (21% of subscribers)
• "Movie Buffs" (13% of subscribers but 38% of watched movies) should be recognized to retain them as best of the best

Source: EachMovie database.

CASE STUDY: Create PowerPoint slides (Continued)

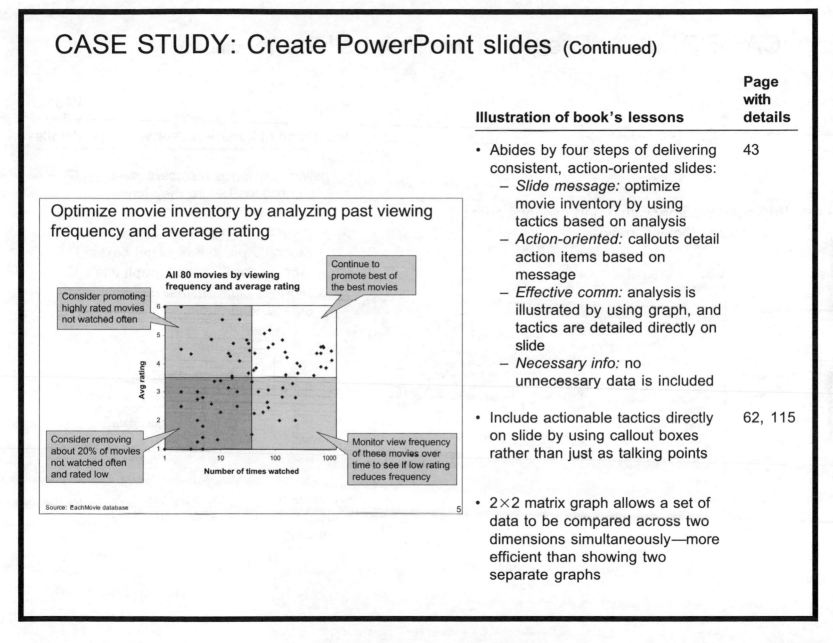

Optimize movie inventory by analyzing past viewing frequency and average rating

Consider promoting highly rated movies not watched often

All 80 movies by viewing frequency and average rating

Continue to promote best of the best movies

Consider removing about 20% of movies not watched often and rated low

Monitor view frequency of these movies over time to see If low rating reduces frequency

Avg rating

Number of times watched

Source: EachMovie database

Illustration of book's lessons	Page with details
• Abides by four steps of delivering consistent, action-oriented slides:	43

– *Slide message:* optimize movie inventory by using tactics based on analysis

– *Action-oriented:* callouts detail action items based on message

– *Effective comm:* analysis is illustrated by using graph, and tactics are detailed directly on slide

– *Necessary info:* no unnecessary data is included

• Include actionable tactics directly on slide by using callout boxes rather than just as talking points 62, 115

• 2×2 matrix graph allows a set of data to be compared across two dimensions simultaneously—more efficient than showing two separate graphs

Improve inventory within genres since some genres have more efficient* movies

	Average views per movie within genre	% of all movies
Action	401	14%
Horror	295	4%
Animation	293	3%
Family	207	7%
Romance	189	7%
Comedy	151	19%
Thriller	103	5%
Drama	103	24%
Classic	29	7%
Art/Foreign	23	10%

Focus on improving genres with lower average viewing efficiency, especially Comedy and Drama

*Efficiency defined by views per movie.
Source: EachMovie database.

6

Illustration of book's lessons — Page with details

- Answers audience members' data-slide questions before they have chance to ask: 77
  - *Insights I care about?* starburst 113
  - *Key data points?* highlight boxes 114
  - *What is data?* bolded graph title 128
  - *Which is biggest/smallest?* data organized in order: 117

Average views per movie within genre	
Action	401
Animation	293
Art/Foreign	23
Classical	29
Comedy	151
Drama	103
Family	207
Horror	295
Romance	189
Thriller	103

This version, in alphabetical order, takes longer to digest data

- Starburst highlights actionable insight directly on slide and is eye-catching 62

CASE STUDY: Create PowerPoint slides (Continued)

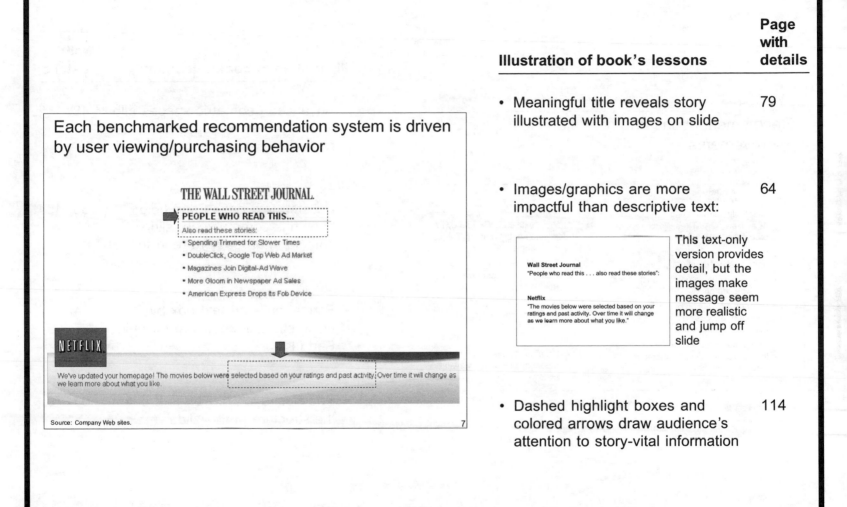

Illustration of book's lessons	Page with details
• Meaningful title reveals story illustrated with images on slide	79
• Images/graphics are more impactful than descriptive text:	64
• Dashed highlight boxes and colored arrows draw audience's attention to story-vital information	114

Within the slide:

Each benchmarked recommendation system is driven by user viewing/purchasing behavior

THE WALL STREET JOURNAL

PEOPLE WHO READ THIS...
Also read these stories:
• Spending Trimmed for Slower Times
• DoubleClick, Google Top Web Ad Market
• Magazines Join Digital-Ad Wave
• More Gloom in Newspaper Ad Sales
• American Express Drops Its Fob Device

NETFLIX

We've updated your homepage! The movies below were selected based on your ratings and past activity. Over time it will change as we learn more about what you like.

Source: Company Web sites. 7

This text-only version provides detail, but the images make message seem more realistic and jump off slide

Wall Street Journal
"People who read this . . . also read these stories":

Netflix
"The movies below were selected based on your ratings and past activity. Over time it will change as we learn more about what you like."

CASE STUDY: Create PowerPoint slides (Continued)

	Page with details
Illustration of book's lessons	

Recommendations and next steps to implement improvements

Recommendations	Next steps
• Initiate direct marketing campaigns to re-activate "One-Time Watchers" and recognize "Movie Buffs"	1. Work with creative agency to develop direct marketing campaigns
• Manage inventory by removing underviewed, poorly rated movies	
• Promote highly rated movies that are not watched often	2. Remove underperforming movies from Web site
• Balance distribution of movies across genres and focus on improving the average viewing efficiency	3. Purchase new movies in underperforming genres
• Use a movie recommendation model to make suggestions to increase viewing frequency	4. Create a movie recommendation model by using past viewing history

Source: Team analysis.

8

- Advanced geometric shapes allow you to deliver two separate but related messages on a single slide 42, 162

- Bulleted text boxes and bold headings communicate slide's content in an easy-to-read format 63, 154

- Format bulleted text box by using shortcut keyboard tricks in Part III 144

- See illustration of how to create the structure of this slide 69–70

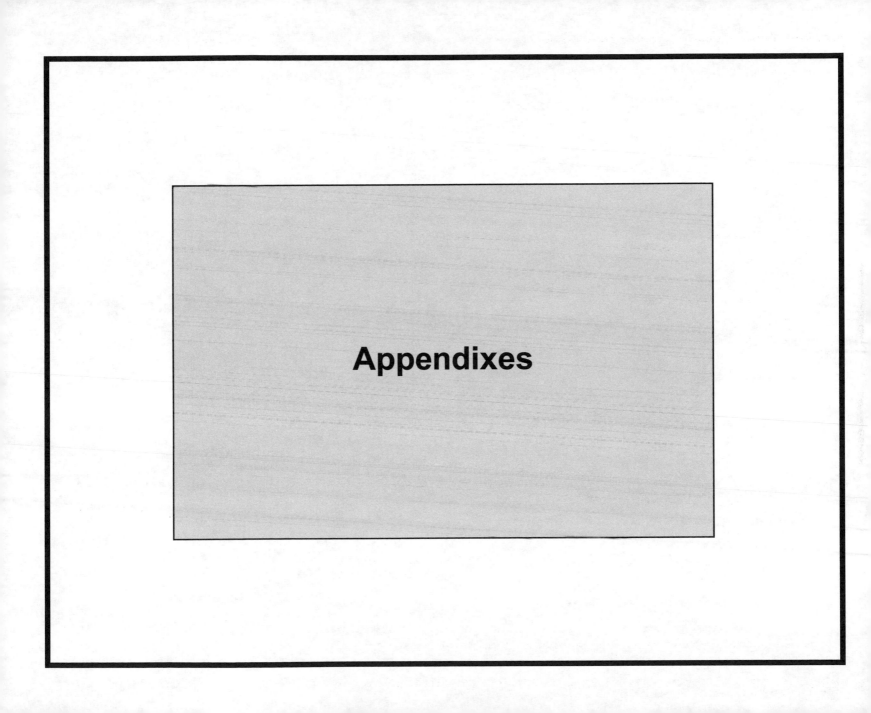

Appendixes

Appendixes

Simple techniques to plan, design, and deliver presentations that get results

Appendix: Contents

Appendix A PowerPoint 2007 Version Screenshots

PowerPoint 2007: Creating graphs in Excel from Chapter 7

Note: Instructions for creating graphs in Chapter 7 are relatively consistent between Office versions. The primary difference is that Excel 2007 does not use the "Chart Wizard." Use the illustration below to create different types of graphs. Then follow the formatting instructions in Chapter 7 to make graphs presentation-ready.

Create graphs in Excel 2007:
- In Excel 2007, go to "Insert" tab
- Select data you want to include in graph
- In "Charts," select the graph type you want
- Click on specific graph from the drop-down menu (remember, do not use 3-D graphs as they are more difficult to read)
- Once graph is created, use formatting and copy/paste instructions from Chapter 7 to paste graph into PowerPoint

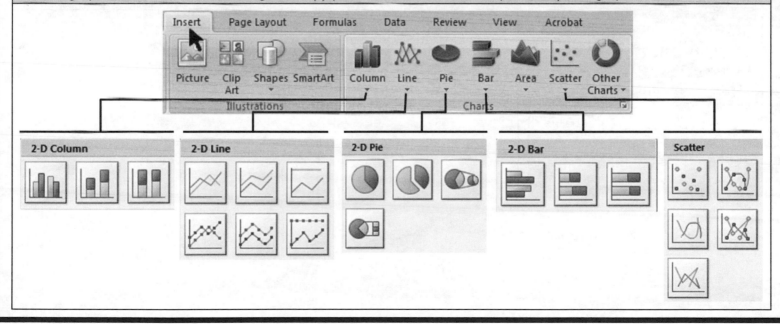

PowerPoint 2007: Creating and editing text boxes

Insert text box:
- Go to "Home" tab
- Click on "Shapes" icon
- Click "Text Box" in "Basic Shapes"

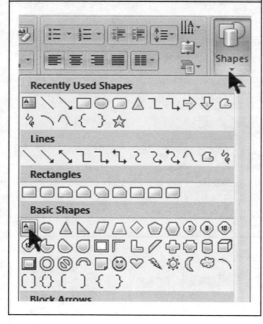

Format text style and alignment:
- Go to "Home" tab
- Select text box
- Click styling and alignment icons in Font or Paragraph

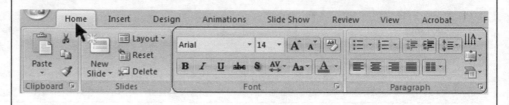

PowerPoint Presentations That Sell

PowerPoint 2007: Formatting text style and line spacing

Format text style and alignment:
- Right click on selected text box
- Click "Format Text Effects…"
- Adjust the following:
  - "Vertical alignment": "Top"
  - Click "Resize shape to fit text"
  - Internal margins: set to "0"
  - Check "Wrap text in shape"
- Hit "Close"

Change line spacing:
- Go to "Home" tab
- Select text box
- In "Paragraph," click icon in bottom right corner to open dialog box
- In "Paragraph" dialog box that appears, use "After:" option to increase space
- "After:" option (set at 3–6 pts) is most commonly used
- Note: PowerPoint 2007 uses "pt" rather than "lines" in the 2003 version.

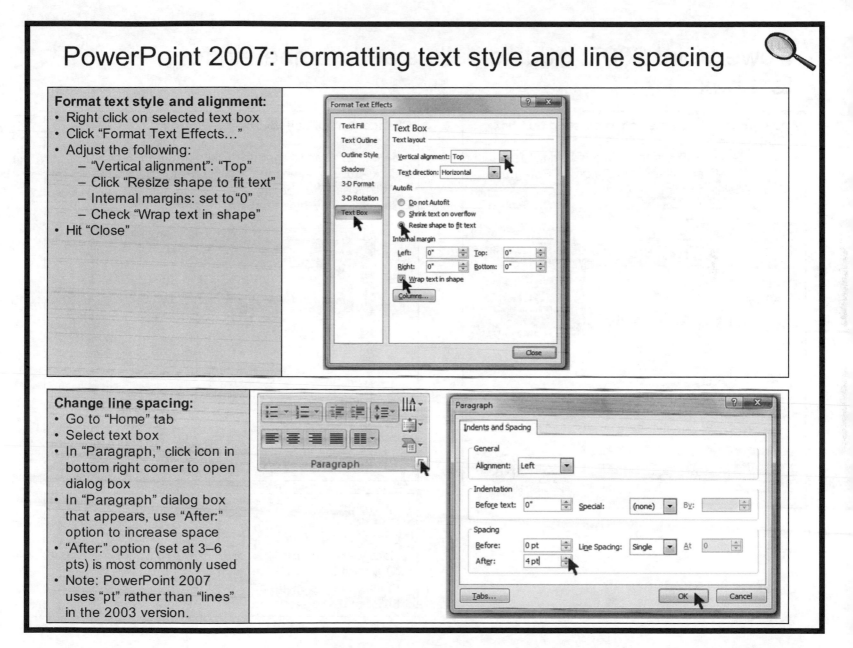

PowerPoint 2007: Adding bullets and numbering to text box

Add bullets and numbering to existing text box*:
- Go to "Home" tab
- Select text box to add bullets/numbering
- Click "Bullets and Numbering" icon in "Paragraph"
- Select desired bullet/numbering

Change type of bullets and numbering:
- Go to "Home" tab
- Select text box to change bullets and numbering
- Click "Bullets/Numbering" icon in "Paragraph" and click "Bullets and Numbering. . ."
- Select desired bullet/numbering and hit "OK"

Open ruler
- Go to "View" tab
- Check "Ruler"
- Note: See Chapter 10, "Quick Hit FAQs," for steps to make words inside a bulleted text box line up

*See previous pages for instructions for creating text boxes.

PowerPoint 2007: Creating and editing shapes

Create shapes:
- Go to "Home" tab
- Click "Shapes" icon in "Drawing"
- Select desired shape (see below for most common)

Change shape background/fill color:
- Go to "Home" tab
- Click "Shape Fill" drop-down menu in "Drawing"
- Select desired shape color

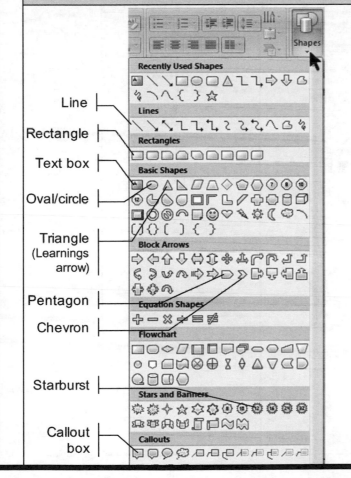

Line
Rectangle
Text box
Oval/circle
Triangle
(Learnings arrow)
Pentagon
Chevron
Starburst
Callout box

PowerPoint 2007: Formatting line styling

Change line style:
- Go to "Home" tab
- Select line(s) you want to change
- Click "Shape Outline" in "Drawing"
- Select desired line color, weight, dash, or arrow style by using drop-down menus

PowerPoint Presentations That Sell

PowerPoint 2007: Arranging, aligning, and rotating shapes

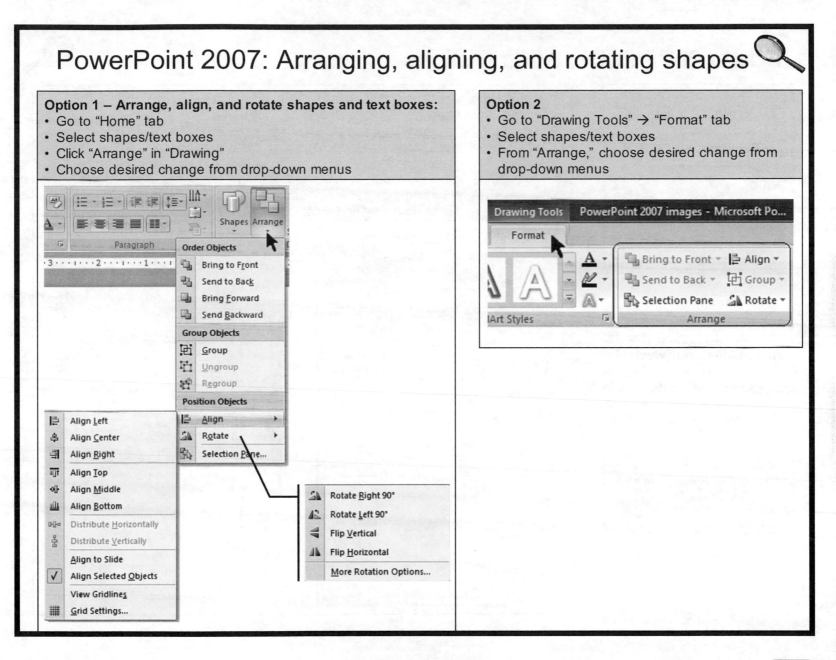

Option 1 – Arrange, align, and rotate shapes and text boxes:
- Go to "Home" tab
- Select shapes/text boxes
- Click "Arrange" in "Drawing"
- Choose desired change from drop-down menus

Option 2
- Go to "Drawing Tools" → "Format" tab
- Select shapes/text boxes
- From "Arrange," choose desired change from drop-down menus

PowerPoint 2007: Adding slides

Insert new slide:
- Go to "Home" tab
- Click on "New Slide" icon
- Alternatively, click Ctrl+M

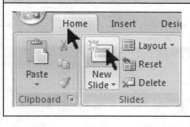

Open Slide Sorter view:
- Go to "View" tab
- Click on "Slide Sorter" icon

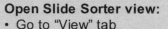

Insert existing slide from existing presentation:
- In new presentation, go to "Home" tab
- Open "Slide Sorter" view by going to "View" tab and clicking on "Slide Sorter" icon
- Click on "New Slide" drop-down menu and click on "Reuse Slides . . ." icon
- Click "Browse" and open the existing presentation file you want to copy from
- Select slide(s) you want (Note: to maintain formatting of existing slides, check "Keep source formatting" box at the bottom)
- Note: inserting slides from existing presentations is a great way to save time!

PowerPoint Presentations That Sell

PowerPoint 2007: Change slide background (Slide Master)

Change slide background (i.e., Slide Master):
- Go to "View" tab
- Click on "Slide Master" icon
- In Slide Master, go to "Design" tab
- Click "Background Styles" icon
- Select style from drop-down menu (remember: keep slide background SIMPLE)
- To insert slide number, go to "Insert" tab and click on "Slide Number" icon

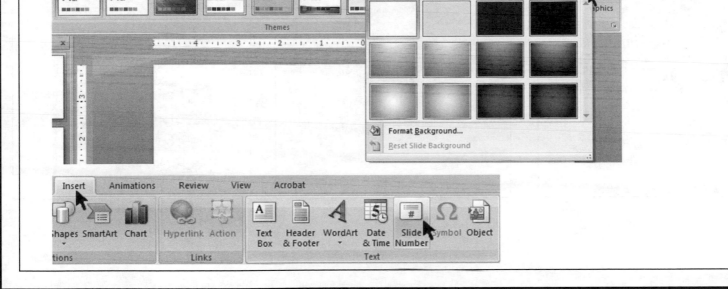

PowerPoint 2007: Miscellaneous:
Creating table; inserting image; paste special

Insert table:
- Go to "Insert" tab
- Click on "Table" icon
- Select size of table (remember to include one column and one row for the labels)
- See Chapter 10, "Quick Hit FAQs," for table formatting instructions once table is created

Insert image:
- Copy/save image file(s) (files with extensions .jpg, .gif, .tif, etc.) in the folder where your PowerPoint presentation is saved
- Go to "Insert" tab
- Click on "Picture" icon
- Locate your saved image in insert

Use paste special:
- After copying image/graph, go to "Home" tab
- Click on "Paste" drop-down menu
- Click "Paste Special . . ."
- Select "Picture (Windows Metafile)" and hit OK

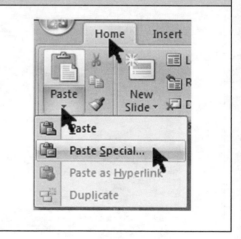

PowerPoint 2007: Using custom animation

Adding custom animation:
- Follow guidance in Chapter 10, "Quick Hit FAQs," for recommendations on how to use custom animation
- Select text boxes/shapes to animate
- Go to "Animations" tab and click "Custom Animation" in "Animations"
- Add animation effects, as detailed in Chapter 10, by clicking "Add Effect" button and selecting desired effect

Appendix A

Appendix B Example Storyboard for Chapter 3

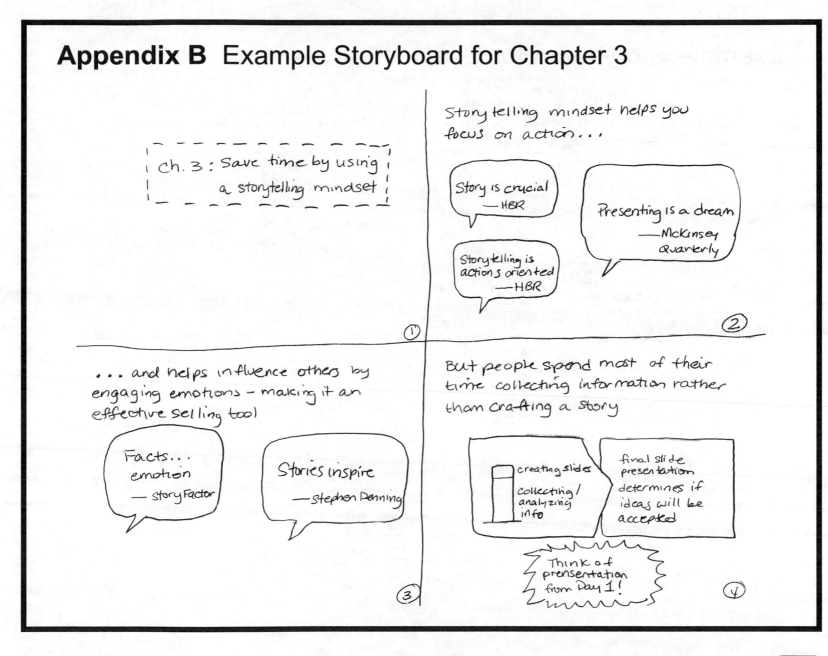

Example Storyboard for Chapter 3 (Continued)

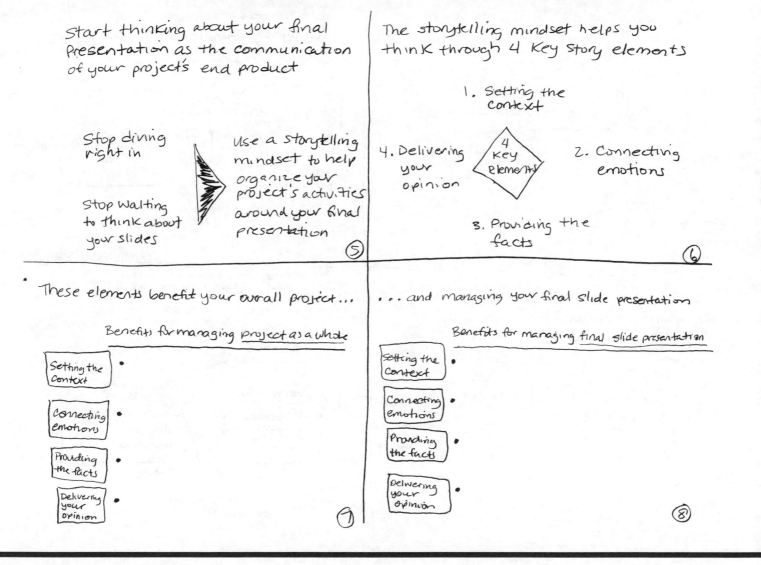

Start thinking about your final presentation as the communication of your project's end product

Stop diving right in

Stop waiting to think about your slides

Use a storytelling mindset to help organize your project's activities around your final presentation ⑤

The storytelling mindset helps you think through 4 key story elements

1. Setting the context
4. Delivering your opinion
   4 Key elements
2. Connecting emotions
3. Providing the facts ⑥

These elements benefit your overall project...

Benefits for managing project as a whole

Setting the Context •
Connecting emotions •
Providing the facts •
Delivering your opinion • ⑦

... and managing your final slide presentation

Benefits for managing final slide presentation

Setting the Context •
Connecting emotions •
Providing the facts •
Delivering your opinion • ⑧

PowerPoint Presentations That Sell

Example Storyboard for Chapter 3 (Continued)

Now you can use your story to structure your project's activities

Storytelling mindset ➤ Agendicize your project ➤ Collect info & analyze ➤ Revisit assumptions

⑨

Begin by Identifying your projects objective

Type of presentation	Details	Example objectives
Selling	• • •	• Identify opportunities • Request funding • Create business plan
Sharing	• •	• Detail new trends • Update on performance to date

⑩

Next, identify who your audience is

Difficult to sell ideas if you don't Know who audience is

Ways to Identify
•
•
•

⑪

... and think through the needs of your primary & secondary audiences

	Description	Questions to think through
Primary audience	• •	• •
Secondary audience	• •	• •

⑫

Example Storyboard for Chapter 3 (Continued)

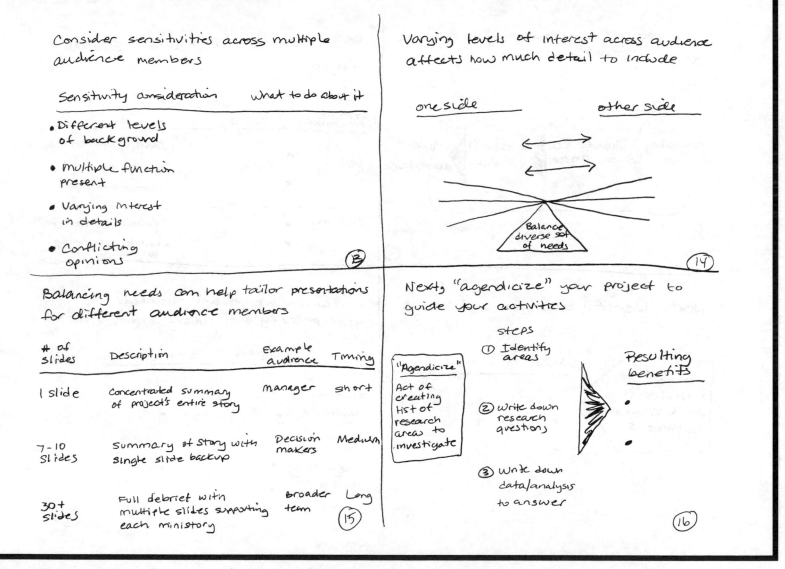

Consider sensitivities across multiple audience members

Sensitivity consideration   what to do about it

- Different levels of background
- multiple function present
- Varying interest in details
- Conflicting opinions

(13)

Varying levels of interest across audience affects how much detail to include

one side   other side

Balance diverse set of needs

(14)

Balancing needs can help tailor presentations for different audience members

# of slides	Description	Example audience	Timing
1 slide	Concentrated summary of project's entire story	manager	short
7-10 slides	summary of story with single slide backup	Decision makers	Medium
30+ slides	Full debrief with multiple slides supporting each ministry	Broader team	Long

(15)

Next, "agendicize" your project to guide your activities

steps

① Identify areas

"Agendicize"
Act of creating list of research areas to investigate

② write down research questions

③ write down data/analysis to answer

Resulting benefits

(16)

Example Storyboard for Chapter 3 **(Continued)**

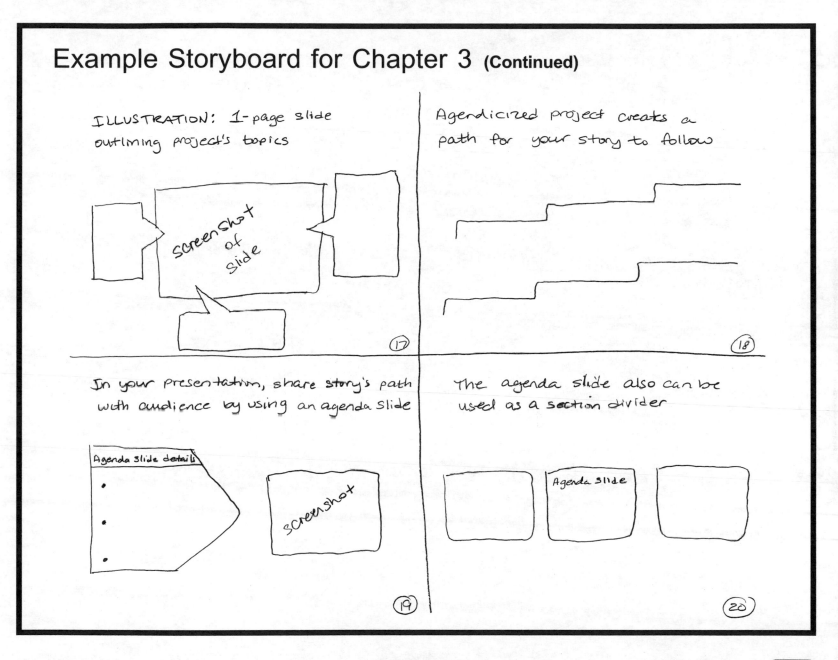

Index

Boxes (*See specific types of boxes, such as* text boxes)

Bullets/numbering:
adding, 70, 154
adjusting space between text and, 156
bulleted list vs. smart slide structure, 54
changing, 155
in PowerPoint 2007, 206
reformatting, keyboard shortcuts for, 144
smart slide structure, 54, 58, 63, 70
text:
case study, 190, 193, 197
creating, in smart slide structure, 63
smart slide structure, 58

C

Callout boxes:
creating, in smart slide structure, 62
emphasizing principles, 115
Callout icons in book, 5
Categories of information, smart slide structure, 57
Category boxes:
case study, 193
creating, in smart slide structure, 61, 70
Changing:
background, 163
bullet reformatting, 144

bullets/numbering in text boxes, 155
graph reformatting, 97, 103
size of text boxes, 152
text box reformatting, 145
Chart Wizard in Excel, creating data-driven graphs, 97, 100–102
Circles, keyboard shortcuts for, 143
Citations on slide, 173
Clutter reduction on slides, 111, 121–127
Color:
background, 121, 163
of data bars in bar graphs, 194
emphasizing principles, 115
line color, 163
of shapes, 163
smart slide structure, 64
of text, in text boxes, 153
Columns and column graphs:
adjusting column width, 122
case study, 190, 194
as comparison graph, 84
as distribution graph, 85
double bar graphs, 84, 86
3-D vs. basic columns, 127
time graphs, 86
Combined graphs, selecting and presenting, 87
Commas, formatting principles, 125
Common topics within categories, 57
Communication (*See* Effective communication; *specific topics*)
Comparison message, selecting and presenting, 82–85, 88

Conceptual approach to presentation, 5–6
Conflicting opinions, as audience sensitivity, 27
Connecting to emotions, as key story element, 20–22
Context setting, as key story element, 20–22
Copy and paste:
from Excel:
creating data-driven graphs, 97, 104, 203
tables, 170–172
from existing presentation, 137, 177
objects, with keyboard shortcuts, 141
text boxes, 159
Criticisms of PowerPoint general usage, 7

D

Dashed boxes:
case study, 197
emphasizing principles, 114
Dashed lines:
creating, 164
emphasizing principles, 120
Data accents, 110, 119–120
Data and analysis needed, 30–31
Data-driven graphs, 95–104
"emphasizing" and "formatting" principles, 96
PowerPoint 2007, 203
from scratch, 95, 97–104

Index

About the Author

Adam B. Cooper currently works as a consultant at a global management consulting firm. He previously worked as a marketing manager for leading consumer goods and retail companies. As a business professional and an MBA student at the Ross School of Business at the University of Michigan, he exhibited special talents driven by his extensive use of PowerPoint to present ideas and recommendations. This book was inspired by questions the author received from people seeking to understand how to use PowerPoint to sell their ideas. Those questions prompted Adam to put into writing a set of simple lessons to help business professionals and students rethink their approach not only to structuring slides but to creating presentations that empower them to sell their ideas.